KETOGENIC MEDITERRANEAN DIET

Ketogenic
Mediterranean
Diet

**Delicious Low-Carb Recipes for
Heart Health and Longevity**

Jason Sanna

 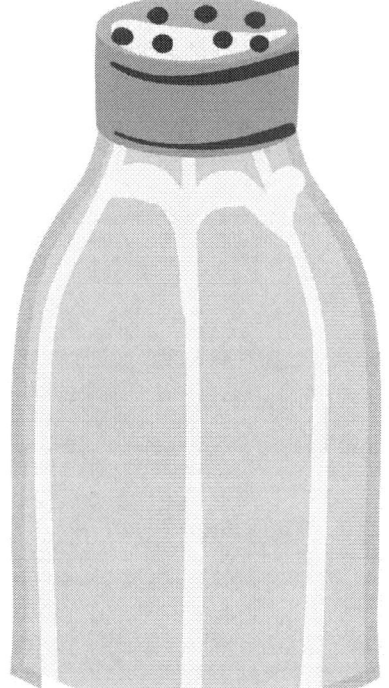

CONTENTS

THE KETO MEDITERRANEAN DIET

I grew up in a typical American home, with my dad going to the office every day and my mom staying at home to take care of us children. What I appreciated the most about my childhood was that my mom did all she could to make sure we learned to love healthy eating. Of course, we also ate processed foods at home and in fast food restaurants every once in a while, but that's the keyword -- "once in a while."

Perhaps that's the reason my relationship with food began to sour when I was able to earn my own money. I felt that I wasn't really able to enjoy the same types of food my peers enjoyed growing up. You know -- hotdogs, burgers, fries, ice cream. So, when I had my first job, I would treat myself to all the food I found pleasurable every time I received my salary. Fast food, prepackaged food, snack bars, -- I began living on these, not realizing that they would slowly take their toll on my health.

I'm into sports, I tell you, and I'm fit overall. But over time, my bad eating habits began taking effect. At 5'10", I weighed 195lbs. I wasn't that fat, but I knew I was overweight. For the sake of my wife and my then two-year old son, I decided I had to eat healthier. That's when I began researching on different diets. I've heard about the Mediterranean diet from my dad back in 2008. He mentioned his doctor advised him to try it after he had undergone goiter surgery. It wasn't until 2013, though, that I actually tried to find out what the Mediterranean diet was.

I hesitated at first, thinking that it would really take a hit on our finances, considering how expensive healthy diets can be. But then I realized that if I'm going to go on the Mediterranean diet, I would have to stop spending money on unhealthy foods, and so I decided to do it. After just a couple of months, I felt a huge change in my overall health. For one, I felt an improvement in my mood. I had an accident in 2012 where I hit my head hard on concrete while playing a game of basketball. One of the effects of my concussion was that I became moodier.

I also began to lose weight and maintain it at the right numbers. A digestive problem I always struggled with also improved. Overall, I really didn't have any problems with the Mediterranean diet, only that the wide variety of foods that it allowed me to eat sometimes caused me to eat more than I should.

It was around that time that a friend of mine introduced me to the Keto diet. I was surprised at first that it focused heavily on high-fat foods, but when my friend explained the reason, I was convinced. I didn't actually try the diet, although I did a lot of research on it. I also wondered if I could try to merge it with the Mediterranean diet that I was already doing. To my surprise, it's actually been done already in 2008 by some Spanish researchers. The diet was named the Spanish Ketogenic Mediterranean Diet.

As was my practice, I began researching more about my new discovery. It's only been a year and a half since the first time I tried the Keto Mediterranean diet and I would say that it has really worked well for me, particularly in helping me maintain a healthy lifestyle and keeping my mind and body replenished at the same time.

This book is a result of the time I spent studying and applying the Keto Mediterranean diet. I hope the information here helps you as it has helped me.

Yours in good health,

Jason Sanna

INTRODUCTION

For years, the Mediterranean diet has been considered the number one overall diet. It's been widely recognized as the best diet for weight loss, as well as for overall health. Compared to the typical diet of the West that's filled with highly-processed foods, the Mediterranean diet is plant-based, making it safe and effective and relied upon by those who have tried and tested it.

Meanwhile, more and more radically unconventional diets are coming out nowadays. They are known to have a greater potential to deliver results. However, most of the changes that come with such diets are somewhat drastic, resulting in increased health risk for some people. One such diet is the Keto diet.

The Keto diet is a very low-carb, high-fat diet that can be compared to the Atkins diet. It is backed up by an overabundance of research claiming that this unconventional approach can help with a range of health conditions including Alzheimer's disease, Parkinson's disease, diabetes, and obesity. However, while many followers of the Keto diet swear by its benefits, there are some individuals whose health may actually worsen by following a diet such as this one.

This is where the Keto Mediterranean diet comes in. Both the Mediterranean and the Keto diet has its advantages and drawbacks. When combined into one, however, most of the drawbacks of each of the two diets are eliminated. This leaves dieters with a way of consuming food that will not only improve health, but every aspect of life.

Before we examine the Keto Mediterranean diet in detail, let's first unpack the principles foundational to each of the two diets. It's only by having a deep understanding of the Mediterranean and the Keto diets that you will learn to establish the right strategies to meet your dietary goals.

THE MEDITERRANEAN DIET

The Mediterranean diet is currently ranked first as the best overall diet, so it's only right to introduce it first. Inspired by the eating habits of people from Greece and Italy, the diet first gained popularity in the 1960s when researchers made an observation that few people in Mediterranean countries suffered and died from coronary heart disease compared to those living in other parts of the world, particularly those following a typical western diet.

It was the University of Minnesota professor, Ancel Keys, PhD, who first did intensive research on the impact of the Mediterranean diet to overall health, publishing several studies in the span of fifty years. His Seven Countries Study involving 13,000 middle-aged men from Finland, Greece, Italy, Japan, Netherlands, the United States, and then-Yugoslavia discovered that men from Crete experienced significantly lower rates of heart disease compared to their counterparts. The study concluded that this lower heart disease rate is directly linked to the "poor man's diet" after World War II, which mainly included fruits and vegetables, as well as beans and fish.

There is no single definition of what a Mediterranean diet is. Nevertheless, it is traditionally known to consist mainly of fruits, vegetables, beans, whole grains, nuts, seeds, fish, and olive oil. In studies, what is typically considered as an authentic Mediterranean diet is one that consists of at least 50% of daily calories coming from carbohydrates, at least 25% of calories coming from fat (unsaturated fats, in particular), and protein.

Unlike other types of diet, the Mediterranean diet isn't too strict when it comes to consuming cheese, eggs, and poultry. Yogurt are a part of the diet, too, although all of these should be eaten in moderation. Red meat is also considered, but should be consumed very rarely. On the other hand, added sugars, refined grains, refined oils, processed meat, and highly processed foods are excluded from this diet.

In a nutshell, the Mediterranean diet is one that's mainly plant-based. Meals are built around fruits and vegetables, as well as herbs, whole grains, beans, and nuts. Seafood, as well as dairy and poultry are also central to it. And instead of saturated and trans fats, healthy fats are the priority for this diet, with olive oil being the primary source of added fat. Olive oil is a good source of monounsaturated fat, which, along with nuts and seeds, has been found to reduce total cholesterol levels.

Fatty fish, too, are a mainstay in the Mediterranean diet. Albacore tuna, herring, lake trout, mackerel, salmon, and sardines are a huge part of the diet due to their high omega-3 fatty acid content. This relatively simple concept of the Mediterranean diet is what makes it a favorite of many. Not to mention the fact that it's supported by a plethora of research.

BENEFITS OF MEDITERRANEAN DIET

Since the publication of Key's study, hundreds of other studies have been done documenting the benefits of observing the Mediterranean diet. Some of the benefits highlighted included the following:

- Lower mortality rate
- Lower blood pressure and LDL cholesterol levels
- Lower risks of type 2 diabetes
- Lower risks of heart disease and cancer
- Lower risks of Alzheimer's disease
- Reduced incidence of heart attack and stroke
- Improved cognitive function

It's Good For The Heart

As mentioned already, the Mediterranean diet is found to be highly beneficial to heart health. It has been linked to decreased risk of heart problems and stroke, and is associated with better heart health. The reason is that the diet is abundant in foods that are rich in heart-healthy omega-3 fatty acids. Nuts, olive oil, some fruits and vegetables, and of course, seafood -- these are rich in omega-3s that helps in the reduction of triglycerides, lowering of blood pressure, and raising of HDL cholesterol levels.

It Improves Brain Health

It's also the omega-3s in foods contained in the Mediterranean diet that helps in improving brain function and overall health. A decline in brain function is an inevitable part of aging, but several studies have discovered that regular consumption of foods rich in omega-3 fatty acids may help lessen age-related mental decline. There are also studies suggesting that omega-3 may help delay the onset of Alzheimer's diseases, especially when it's still in its early stages.

It Helps With Depression

A research published in 2018 reveals that eating a diet rich in fruits, vegetables, nuts, and fish could help lower an individual's risk of depression. The research evaluated over 41 studies done on the topic and discovered a huge link between a person's diet and their risk of developing depression. According to the research, strictly following a Mediterranean diet helps lower the risk of being diagnosed with depressed by up to 33%. Other studies explain that carotenoids found in spinach, kale, and eggs has been shown to promote good bacteria in the gut, which in turn, boosts the mood.

It Can Regulate Blood Sugar Levels

The uniqueness of the Mediterranean diet lies on the fact that it's big on healthy carbs and whole grains. When you consume complex whole grain carbs, such as wheat berries, quinoa, and buckwheat, you're actually helping keep your blood sugar at a healthy level. This even helps with your overall energy so that you don't get tired easily.

It Promotes Healthy Weight Management

Followers of the Mediterranean diet do not promote it as a means to lose weight. In fact, it's possible to follow this diet and still not have a healthy weight. However, it cannot be denied that eating mostly fruits, vegetables, and healthy fats will most likely help you lose excess weight. In most cases, it's because of the high fiber content in the diet that helps in managing fullness. When you eat foods that are high in fiber, you feel more satiated, and this helps with weight loss and metabolism. The main key here is the replacement of simple carbohydrates with foods rich in fiber -- fruits, legumes, beans, and green, leafy vegetables.

It Promotes Healthy Digestive System

Another important benefit of the Mediterranean diet is that it's good for your gut. One study found that following the diet helps promote a higher population of good bacteria in their digestive system. Compared to eating mostly traditional Western diet, following a Mediterranean diet rich in plant-based foods increased the number of beneficial bacteria, particularly Lactobacillus which are mostly probiotic, in the gut by around 7 percent. Not bad.

It Is Linked To Prolonged Lifespan

It's not surprising that the Mediterranean diet is linked to longevity. A Harvard study published in 2014 concluded that the diet may help protect the telomeres, the caps found at the end of each strand of DNA. Telomere length is a biomarker of aging, with shorter telomeres being associated with lower life expectancy. Not only that, but it's also linked to higher rates of developing chronic health problems. In the study, telomere measurements of over 4,000 women were analyzed. The researchers concluded that those who followed a Mediterranean diet had longer telomeres. It also concluded that even a slight change in diet made a significant difference.

While the Mediterranean diet does have a number of benefits and advantages, it is not a magic pill. It may be good for overall health improvement, but there are other aspects of health that may not benefit from it. On the other hand, studies suggest that there are other diets that can deliver where the Mediterranean diet can't. One of which is the Keto diet.

THE KETO DIET

There are many different ways the Keto diet can be defined. In the simplest sense, it is a high-fat, low-carb, moderate-protein diet that was first conceptualized as a form of treatment for a number of epilepsy cases during the early 20th century. It's not enough to describe a Keto diet simply as a high-fat or low-carb diet, though, since there are other diets that can be described in a similar fashion.

The best way to think of a Keto diet is that if you restrict carbohydrates to the point that it allows you to enter and remain in ketosis[1], then you're on a Keto diet. Of course, there are other details involved, but that's straightforward as it can get.

Now, you might be wondering what ketosis is. It's actually a metabolic state that's characterized by raised levels of ketones in your body. Ketones are byproducts of the breakdown of fatty acids and are used by the body as fuel. In order for the body to produce ketones, there has to be a continual trigger of a process called ketogenesis. One way this happens is when a person has diabetes. A healthy way to trigger ketogenesis, however, is by limiting consumption of carbohydrates.

And yes, Keto is actually short for ketogenesis, and that's why this low-carb diet is referred to as the "ketogenic diet," with the primary goal of limiting carbs so that your body stimulates ketogenesis and enter ketosis. In order to enter this unique metabolic state, you need to limit or altogether avoid high-carb foods, such as grans (wheat, rice, cereal, corn), sugar (both natural and artificial), and tubers (potatoes, cassava, yams).

Meanwhile, you will need to get most of your calories from healthy fat-rich foods like meat (fish, beef, poultry, lamb, eggs), low-carb veggies (broccoli, kale, spinach), high-fat dairy (cheese, cream, butter), nuts and seeds (walnuts, sunflower seeds, macadamias), fats from coconut oil and saturated fats, and some fruits, such as avocado and berries.

It's important to note that when carb or protein consumption are too high, it may impair the production of ketone. This is why it's essential to make sure one is eating 70% fats, 25% protein, and 5% carbs.

While there's not as much research on the benefits of the Keto diet than on the Mediterranean diet, data suggests that the Keto diet can have significant benefits on the health including a decrease in blood sugar, insulin, and hbA1c levels, as well as a reduction in triglyceride levels. The diet has also been found to help optimize blood cholesterol levels and reduce blood pressure levels. And like the Mediterranean diet, it has also been found to be helpful in lowering risks for type 2 diabetes, fatty liver disease, neurological disorders (Alzheimer's, Parkinson's, and epilepsy), and certain types of cancer.

Despite the fact that the Keto diet has been proven to have many significant health benefits, just like the Mediterranean diet, it doesn't work like a magic pill. In fact, there are potential downsides of the Keto diet that are often criticized by many, including the fact that the increased intake of saturated fat will eventually increase cholesterol levels, leading to many types of heart problems.

---

[1] https://www.medicalnewstoday.com/articles/180858.php

Research admits that this may occur only on a small subset of the population, it can't be denied that the Keto diet optimizes cholesterol levels in the body, plus many other risk factors for cardiovascular disease. This is where the importance of combining the Keto diet and the Mediterranean diet comes in. By combining these two diets, the dilemma of increased cholesterol levels brought about by the Keto diet is dealt with.

THE SIMILARITIES AND DIFFERENCES

The Similarities

In order for us to better understand the Keto Mediterranean diet, we need to first discover the similarities and differences between the two separate diets. It's interesting to note that there are many similarities between the Keto and Mediterranean diets, and when compared to the common diet of many people nowadays, it's clear that the two diets come out superior in terms of health benefits.

Perhaps the most striking similarity between the two diets is that they benefit similar aspects of human health. For instance, both diets are found to help improve crucial biomarkers for health, including blood sugar, blood pressure, triglyceride, and cholesterol levels.

Another similarity is that both diets can provide long-term weight loss benefits. It's true that one can shed more weight the Keto diet in the short-term, but according to studies, both the Keto and the Mediterranean diets provide similar results in the long run, particularly after 12 to 24 months.

Aside from similarities in weight loss benefits, the two diets are also alike in terms of adherence levels. People seem to have the same level of tolerance for both the Keto and the Mediterranean diet. While it would seem that the Keto diet is the more restrictive of the two diets, data suggests that it has the same drop-out rates as the Mediterranean diet and other similar diets. This tells us that adherence to each of these diets and other diets available rely more on individual differences and not simply on how restrictive or not a particular diet is.

Finally, both diets promote clean eating. This means both the Keto and Mediterranean diets focus on consuming whole foods and discourage anything that is heavily processed. This idea alone of prioritizing quality of food consumed is one of the most important factors responsible for the countless benefits both diets offer to human health.

The Differences

While the Keto and Mediterranean diets share a number of similarities, the two diets also have several notable differences. When it comes to carb intake, for instance, the Keto diet focuses on going very low, and that includes unrefined high-carb plant sources. The Mediterranean diet, on the other hand, eliminates refined sugars altogether and highlights healthy fat. Nevertheless, it includes high amount of carbohydrates in moderation, whether it's pastas, whole grain breads, or fruits.

In terms of fat intake, the Keto diet has fat as its primary source of calories. For the Mediterranean diet, the main source of calories is carbs. And while the Mediterranean is not as restrictive to fat compared to other low-fat diets, it is still much lower in fat compared to the Keto diet.

And speaking of fat, the type of fat consumed is another difference between the two diets. With the Mediterranean diet, for instance, the emphasis is on natural unsaturated fats coming from fish and plant-based oils. With Keto, there is no problem including an abundant amount of saturated and unsaturated fats to your diet.

THE ADVANTAGES OF DRAWBACKS OF THE KETO DIET

The following are the advantages of the Keto diet over a typical Mediterranean diet:

- Higher potential to lower insulin, blood, sugar, hbA1c, and triglyceride levels.
- Higher potential to increase HDL or "good" cholesterol.
- Has been proven to aid in the treatment of disorders like Alzheimer's disease and Parkinson's disease, as well as PCOS, epilepsy, type 2 diabetes, and several types of cancer.
- Eliminates foods that encourage binge-eating.
- Reduces appetite.
- Reduces calorie intake.
- More sustainable long-term diet for most people.

Meanwhile, here are the potential disadvantages of the same diet:

- Causes many people to experience keto flu[2] during the first few days of trying out the diet for the first time.
- Causes greater risk for deficiency in vitamins and minerals if not properly formulated.
- May not be the best option for individuals suffering from hypothyroid or adrenal-related conditions.
- May cause individuals with familial hypercholesterolemia to experience undesirable changes in cholesterol levels upon increasing their consumption of saturated fat.

THE ADVANTAGES OF DRAWBACKS OF THE MEDITERRANEAN DIET

The following are the advantages of the Mediterranean diet over the Keto diet:

- Comes with more research to support its health benefits, making it the safer option.
- Has been proven to significantly reduce cardiovascular disease.
- Prioritizes foods that are more environmentally-friendly by promoting the consumption of whole plant foods and discouraging intake of red meat and animal products.
- Has been found to significantly reduce LDL cholesterol levels in the body.
- Promotes lesser risk for vitamin and mineral deficiency by allowing for the intake of a wide variety of foods.

Despite the many advantages of the Mediterranean diet, it has some downsides, too:

Most of the wide variety of foods it incorporates are easier for many to overeat, leading to higher chances of fat gain.

---

[2] https://www.health.harvard.edu/blog/what-is-keto-flu-2018101815052

May not be as efficient as the Keto diet in yielding remarkable differences in body composition and blood markers.

THE KETO MEDITERRANEAN DIET: THE BEST OF BOTH WORLDS

We have seen each of the pros and cons of the Keto and Mediterranean diets, and that leaves us with a question: What happens when we combine these two diets? Well, this is the question a 2008 study[3] involving researchers from Spain tried to answer. The prospective study was called the Spanish Ketogenic Mediterranean Diet.

The researchers merged the four major components of the Mediterranean diet: fish, salad, olive oil, and red wine, and included in it an array of both Keto-friendly and Keto-borderline foods. This meant including some of the major principles of KD, which included the following:

- Unlimited Calories
- Olive oil as a major source of fat.
- Green veggies and salads as a major source of carbs
- Fish as a major protein source
- Red wine in moderate amounts

The results of the merging of these two ideal diets were as one would expect. After the study, participants were found to have lost a significant amount of body fat, and their triglyceride, glucose, and blood pressure levels became more normal. In addition, something interesting happened to each of the participant's cholesterol numbers. After the study, there was an increase in their HDL or "good" cholesterol and a reduction in LDL or "bad" cholesterol.

Simply put, the Keto Mediterranean diet attenuated the increase in LDL cholesterol that was considered a common result of following a typical Keto diet, while at the same time keeping the HDL at a healthy level. This is a good indication that restricting carbs and consuming more foods like fish, olive oil, and other foods rich in unsaturated fat may be a fitting game plan for individuals experiencing detrimental cholesterol levels.

This initial study was followed by another one several years later. The researchers did another study similar to the first, but this time exploring the effects of a Keto Mediterranean diet supplemented by herbal extracts.[4] After the six-week study, the researchers once again saw the remarkable improvement in cholesterol levels, including the reduction in total cholesterol and LDL cholesterol, and an increase in HDL cholesterol.

More recently, another study yielded very similar results, but this time with higher reduction not only in LDL but also in triglycerides and insulin. Researchers also discovered that the diet was able to significantly reduce inflammation levels among the participants.

As the experts predicted, the merging of the Keto and Mediterranean diets yielded very promising results as supported by clinical studies. This is a confirmation that that unique fusion will provide adherents the benefits and advantages of both diets in one.

---

[3] https://www.ncbi.nlm.nih.gov/pubmed/18950537
[4] https://www.ncbi.nlm.nih.gov/pubmed/21992535

WHAT DOES A KETO MEDITERRANEAN DIET LOOK LIKE?

There is no strict definition for what the Keto Mediterranean diet should look like. Even researchers used different variations on their studies. Nevertheless, there are certain key characteristics of the diet combination that we can look at to help us understand what it really means to adhere to a Keto Mediterranean diet.

Low Carbs for Promotion of Ketosis. Stimulation of ketone production starts when total carbs are kept below 35g and net carbs are kept below 25g. Over time, this also allows the body to go through deeper levels of ketosis. Restricting carb intake to this level will help you manage your appetite better, boost weight loss, and reduce your triglycerides, insulin, blood sugar, and hbA1c levels significantly.

Consume Polyunsaturated and Monounsaturated Fats in High Amounts. There are many healthy foods available that will help you achieve this. For instance, you can consume avocados and avocado oil instead of coconut oil and butter. Olive oil is an excellent choice, too. You can also achieve this by eating fish, seafood, and poultry instead of red meat. And instead of snacking on processed foods, focus on nuts, seeds, and even hard cheese. These changes are enough to help increase your consumption of healthy fats that boost cholesterol and triglyceride levels. If you have problems with inflammation, triglyceride, and insulin levels, supplementing with DHA+EPA may also help.

Keto-Friendly Veggies as Main Source of Carbs. It's a must for anyone who wishes to follow a Keto Mediterranean diet to eat plenty of green, leafy, colorful, and cruciferous vegetables. In fact, having them in every meal should be the main goal. Not only do these vegetables contain much-needed vitamins and minerals and fiber, but they also help prevent the flu-like symptoms most people experience when they try to enter ketosis for the first time. Keep in mind, though, that some vegetables may contain higher levels of net carbs. For this reason, be sure to familiarize yourself with low-carb veggies before incorporating any to your diet.

Seafood, Fish, Eggs, and Poultry as Main Source of Protein. These foods are highly rich in protein, as well as in unsaturated fats and other compounds important to the health. Salmon, sardines, and similar fishes, in particular, are some of the best options since they are not only rich in protein but most importantly in omega-3 fatty acids. They're also more sustainable environmentally speaking when compared to other seafood. Aside from these fish, excellent options for protein include pasture-raised poultry and eggs.

Adjust Protein and Fat Intake Based On Individual Needs. The key to an effective Keto Mediterranean diet is to adjust your intake of protein and fat depending on your needs. If you're into bodybuilding, for instance, eating more protein will ensure that you continue building your muscles. Adjusting your fat consumption, on the other hand, will help in managing your weight loss rate. If you're not sure how to fine-tune your protein and fat intake based on your health and lifestyle needs, you can always make use of Keto calculators available online.

THE KETO MEDITERRANEAN DIET FOOD LIST

The Keto Mediterranean diet consists primarily of the following foods:

- Seafood, fish, poultry, eggs
- Olive oil, avocado oil, MCT oil

- Leafy greens, cruciferous vegetables - cauliflower, cabbage, kale, spinach, lettuce, arugula, etc.
- Fruits low in carbs - avocados, tomatoes, olives
- Mediterranean spices - anise, cinnamon, cumin, garlic, lemon juice, lime juice, mint, oregano, paprika, parsley, Spanish saffron, etc.

Meanwhile, here are foods to eat in moderation:

- Saturated fat-rich oils/fats - butter, coconut oil, cheese, animal fats, etc.
- Fruits low in carbs - melon, berries, kiwi, peach
- High-fat dairy - hard cheese, low-carb yogurt (full-fat), heavy cream, etc.
- Red meat - lamb, pork, beef, etc.
- Nuts and seeds - almonds, pistachios, macadamia, brazil nuts, pecans, chia seeds, flaxseeds, etc.

Foods to avoid:

- Tubers - yams, potatoes, cassava, dahlia, etc.
- Fruits - apples, oranges, bananas, etc.
- Sugar - agave, honey, maple syrup, etc.
- Legumes - black beans, peas, lentils, lupins, etc.
- Grains - corn, cereal, rice, wheat, etc.

Foods to eat in limited amounts for lower LDL cholesterol:

Butter

- Coconut oil
- Cream
- Red Meat
- Fatty Cuts

BENEFITS OF THE KETO MEDITERRANEAN DIET

Current studies done on the Keto Mediterranean diet has shown how the combination of the two diets provide more health benefits than either of the diets on its own. Some of these include the following:

- Decrease in inflammation
- Decrease in total cholesterol
- Decrease in LDL cholesterol
- Decrease in triglyceride, insulin, blood sugar, and hbA1c levels
- Decrease in blood pressure levels
- Increase in HDL cholesterol levels
- Significant fat loss

While there are not a good number of studies yet on other benefits of the diet, it's safe to conclude that fusing the Keto and the Mediterranean diets can help adherents improve cardiovascular health and lower mortality rate. In the same manner, it's safe to say that the diet can provide unique benefits of carb restriction and ketosis.

There is one very crucial limitation to the current data we have on the Keto Mediterranean diet, though, and that is the fact that no studies have been done yet comparing the said diet to a standard Mediterranean or Keto diet, as well as other low-fat diets. As a result, it's still difficult to completely determine how notable the differences are between each of the said diets.

Nevertheless, the data we currently have does prove that the Keto Mediterranean diet has the ability to optimize important biomarkers linked to heart problems, type 2 diabetes, and overall health. This goes beyond what a standard Mediterranean or Keto diet can do each on their own.

With future of the Keto Mediterranean diet is very promising, thanks to its many research-backed health benefits. Not only can it provide the benefits of ketosis, but it also has the potential of delivering the heart health benefits of the Mediterranean diet.

There is no question that the key to getting the most out of the Keto Mediterranean diet is to study its principles and apply them correctly. As with any diet, however, it's important that you constantly monitor your health and make sure that you're adhering to a diet that's not only for short-term but one that you can follow as a healthy lifestyle.

Moreover, if after trying the diet for a couple of months and you don't see any improvement in your overall health and wellbeing, you might want to consider other options. What's important is that you don't forget to consult your doctor before trying out any kind of diet change.

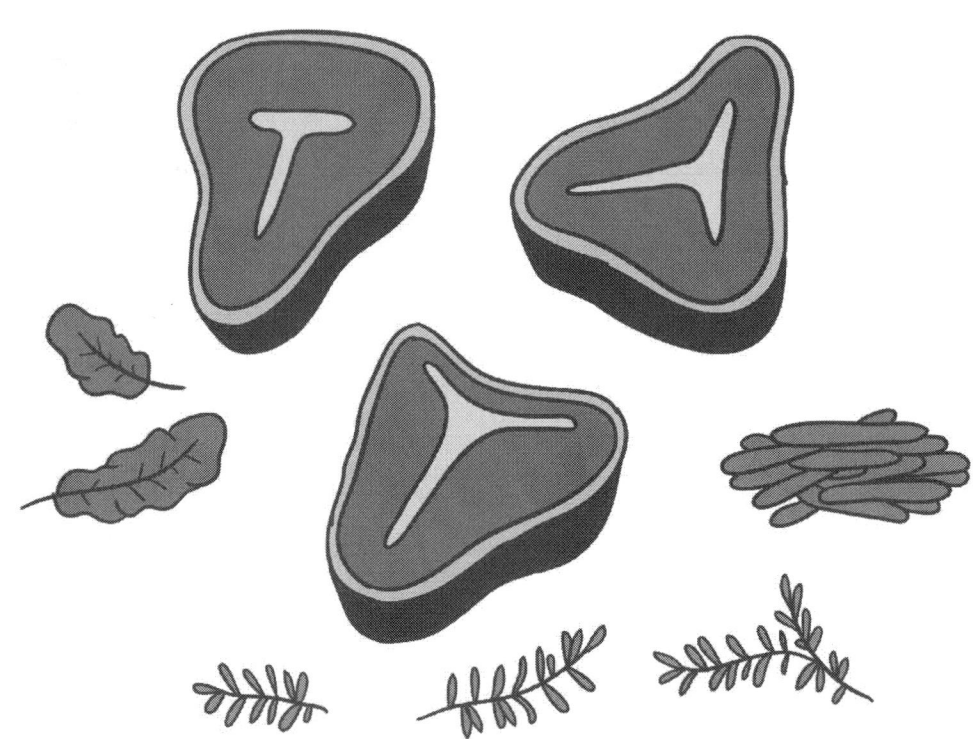

RED MEAT RECIPES

Contents

Lemon Garlic Pork Chops

Serves: 6 / Preparation time: 10 minutes / Cooking time: 8 hours

2 lbs pork chops

1 tsp dried rosemary

1 tsp dried thyme

2 tsp dried parsley

2 tbsp dried oregano

2 tbsp Dijon mustard

1 tbsp garlic, minced

¼ cup fresh lemon juice

3/4 cup olive oil

Pepper

Salt

- Add all ingredients into the slow cooker and mix well.
- Cover and cook on low for 8 hours.
- Serve and enjoy.

Per Serving: Net Carbs: 1.1g; Calories: 714 Total Fat: 63.3 g; Saturated Fat: 17.8g
Protein: 34.6g; Carbs: 2.2g; Fiber: 1.1g; Sugar: 0.3g; Fat 80% / Protein 19% / Carbs 1%

Pork kabobs

Serves: 2 / Preparation time: 10 minutes / Cooking time: 15 minutes

1 lb pork tenderloin, cut into 1-inch pieces

1 onion, cut into 1-inch pieces

2 tbsp olive oil

½ tsp paprika

½ tsp oregano

½ tsp garlic powder

1 tbsp Italian seasoning

Pepper

Salt

- In a mixing bowl, add all ingredients and mix well and place in the refrigerator for overnight.
- Heat grill over medium-high heat.
- Thread marinated pork pieces and onion pieces onto the skewers and grill for 15 minutes. Turn skewers after every 3-4 minutes.
- Serve and enjoy.

Per Serving: Net Carbs: 5.4g; Calories: 493; Total Fat: 24.2g; Saturated Fat: 5.1g
Protein: 60.2g; Carbs: 7g; Fiber: 1.6g; Sugar: 3.2g; Fat 45% / Protein 49% / Carbs 6%

Sweet Pulled Pork

Serves: 8 / Preparation time: 10 minutes / Cooking time: 3 hours 5 minutes

1 ½ lbs pork tenderloin, skinless, boneless, and cut into chunks

1 ½ tbsp Italian seasoning

1 tsp fennel

1 tbsp olive oil

1 tbsp garlic, minced

½ onion, diced

8 oz tomato paste

14.5 oz can tomatoes, diced

1/2 cup light Italian dressing

Pepper

Salt

- Add Italian dressing, Italian seasoning, fennel, tomato paste, and tomatoes into the slow cooker and stir well.

- Season meat with pepper and salt.

- Heat oil in a pan over medium-high heat.

- Add meat to the pan and sear until browned from all the sides. Transfer meat to the slow cooker.

- Add garlic and onion to the same pan and cook for 3-5 minutes. Transfer garlic and onion to the slow cooker. Stir everything well.

- Cover and cook on high for 3 hours.

- Remove meat from slow cooker and shred using a fork. Return shredded meat to the slow cooker and stir well.

- Serve and enjoy.

Per Serving: Net Carbs: 6.4g; Calories: 201; Total Fat: 7.8g; Saturated Fat: 1.6g
Protein: 23.4g; Carbs: 8.5g; Fiber: 2.1g; Sugar: 4.7g; Fat 37% / Protein 49% / Carbs 14%

Flavorful Pork Chops

Serves: 6 / Preparation time: 10 minutes / Cooking time: 10 minutes

6 pork chops, boneless

1 tbsp Italian seasoning

2 tbsp Creole mustard

½ cup zesty Italian dressing

- Add pork chops in a mixing bowl.
- Pour remaining ingredients over pork chops and coat well and place in the refrigerator for 30 minutes.
- Preheat the grill.
- Arrange marinated pork chops on hot grill and cook for 7-10 minutes or until internal temperature reaches to 145 F.
- Serve and enjoy.

Per Serving: Net Carbs: 1.6g; Calories: 333 Total Fat: 27.8g; Saturated Fat: 8.9g
Protein: 18g; Carbs: 1.6g; Fiber: 0g; Sugar: 1.5g; Fat 76% / Protein 22% / Carbs 2%

Italian Pork Roast

Serves: 10 / Preparation time: 10 minutes / Cooking time: 14 hours

5 lbs pork roast, boneless or bone-in

1 tbsp Italian herb mix

5 garlic cloves, cut into slivers

1 tbsp salt

- Using a sharp knife make small cuts all over pork roast then insert garlic slivers into the cuts.
- In a small bowl, mix together Italian herb mix and salt and rub all over pork roast.
- Place pork roast in the slow cooker.
- Cover and cook on low for 14 hours.
- Remove meat from slow cooker and shred using a fork.
- Serve and enjoy.

Per Serving: Net Carbs: 0.7g; Calories: 476; Total Fat: 21.8g; Saturated Fat: 7.8g
Protein: 64.8g; Carbs: 0.7g; Fiber: 0g; Sugar: 0.1g; Fat 43% / Protein 56% / Carbs 1%

Juicy & Tender Pork Tenderloin

Serves: 4 / Preparation time: 10 minutes / Cooking time: 20 minutes

1 ½ lbs pork tenderloin

2 tbsp olive oil

1 tsp ground coriander

1 tsp garlic powder

1 tsp Italian seasoning

¼ tsp pepper

1 tsp sea salt

- Preheat the oven to 204 C/ 400 F.

- Rub pork tenderloin with 1 tablespoon of olive oil.

- Mix together coriander, garlic powder, Italian seasoning, pepper, and salt and rub over pork tenderloin.

- Heat remaining oil in a pan over medium-high heat.

- Add pork tenderloin in hot oil and cook until brown from all the sides.

- Place pork tenderloin on a baking tray and cook in preheated oven for 13-15 minutes. Turn halfway through.

- Slice and serve.

Per Serving: Net Carbs: 0.6g; Calories: 310; Total Fat: 13.3g; Saturated Fat: 3.1g
Protein: 44.7g; Carbs: 0.7g; Fiber: 0.1g; Sugar: 0.3g; Fat 41% / Protein 58% / Carbs 1%

Slow Cooked Pork Roast

Serves: 8 / Preparation time: 10 minutes / Cooking time: 8 hours

3 lbs pork shoulder

½ cup beef broth

½ tsp garlic powder

½ tsp dried rosemary

½ tsp ground sage

½ tsp ground thyme

1 tsp dried basil

1 tsp dried oregano

¼ tsp pepper

1 tsp salt

- Place meat into the slow cooker.
- In a small bowl, mix together garlic powder, rosemary, sage, thyme, basil, oregano, pepper, and salt and sprinkle over meat.
- Add broth around the meat. Cover and cook on low for 8 hours.
- Serve and enjoy.s

Per Serving: Net Carbs: 0.3g; Calories: 501 Total Fat: 36.5g; Saturated Fat: 13.4g
Protein: 40g; Carbs: 0.5g; Fiber: 0.2g; Sugar: 0.1g; Fat 67% / Protein 32% / Carbs 1%

Garlic Beef Roast

Serves: 6 / Preparation time: 10 minutes / Cooking time: 8 hours

2 lbs lean top round beef roast

2 cups beef broth

½ cup red wine

1 tsp red pepper flakes

1 tbsp Italian seasoning

6 garlic cloves, minced

1 onion, sliced

Pepper

Salt

- Season meat with pepper and salt and place into the slow cooker.
- Pour remaining ingredients over meat.
- Cover and cook on low for 8 hours.
- Remove meat from slow cooker and shred using a fork.
- Return shredded meat to the slow cooker and stir well.
- Serve and enjoy.

Per Serving: Net Carbs: 3.5g; Calories: 231; Total Fat: 6.7g; Saturated Fat: 2.3g
Protein: 35.8g; Carbs: 4g; Fiber: 0.5g; Sugar: 1.4g; Fat 29% / Protein 64% / Carbs 7%

Saucy Pork Chops

Serves: 4 / Preparation time: 10 minutes / Cooking time: 6 hours 6 minutes

4 pork chops, bone-in

¼ tsp red pepper flakes

1 tsp Worcestershire sauce

1 tbsp dried Italian seasoning

1 tbsp garlic, minced

½ small onion, chopped

6 oz can tomato paste

1 bell pepper, chopped

14.5 oz can tomatoes, diced

2 tsp olive oil

¼ tsp pepper

1 tsp kosher salt

- Heat oil in a pan over medium-high heat.
- Season pork chops with pepper and salt. Sear pork chops in pan for 2-3 minutes. Turn pork chops to other side and sear for 2-3 minutes more.
- Transfer pork chops to the slow cooker.
- Add remaining ingredients over pork chops.
- Cover slow cooker and cook on low for 6 hours.
- Serve and enjoy.

Per Serving: Net Carbs: 5g; Calories: 313; Total Fat: 23.4g; Saturated Fat: 7.9g
Protein: 19g; Carbs: 6g; Fiber: 1g; Sugar: 3.3g; Fat 68% / Protein 25% / Carbs 7%

Roasted Lamb Chops

Serves: 6 / Preparation time: 10 minutes / Cooking time: 25 minutes

6 lamb chops

1 tbsp sage leaves

10 olives, pitted and chopped

¼ cup butter

3 tbsp olive oil

1 tsp anchovy oil

2 anchovy fillets, minced

1 tbsp garlic, minced

Pepper

Salt

- Preheat the oven to 190 F/ 375 F.

- In a small bowl, whisk together garlic, 1 tablespoon of olive oil, anchovies, pepper, and salt.

- Brush lamb chops with garlic mixture.

- Heat remaining oil in a pan over medium-high heat.

- Once the oil is hot then sear lamb chops in hot oil for 2-3 minutes on each side. Transfer lamb chops to a baking pan.

- Roast in preheated oven for 13-15 minutes. Remove from the oven let it sit for 5 minutes.

- Melt butter in a pan over medium-low heat. Add sage and olives in melted butter and cook for 1-2 minutes.

- Transfer lamb chops onto a serving dish and pour butter olive mixture over lamb chops.

- Serve and enjoy.

Per Serving: Net Carbs: 5.6g; Calories: 401 Total Fat: 30.6g; Saturated Fat: 6g
Protein: 25.6g; Carbs: 5.9g; Fiber: 0.3g; Sugar: 0g; Fat 69% / Protein 26% / Carbs 5%

Tasty Greek Pork Chops

Serves: 8 / Preparation time: 10 minutes / Cooking time: 6 minutes

8 pork chops, boneless

1 tsp ground mustard

2 tsp garlic powder

2 tsp onion powder

4 tsp dried oregano

2 tbsp Worcestershire sauce

3 tbsp fresh lemon juice

¼ cup olive oil

Pepper

Salt

- Whisk together oil, garlic powder, onion powder, oregano, Worcestershire sauce, lemon juice, mustard, pepper, and salt.

- Place pork chops in a baking dish then pour marinade over pork chops and coat well. Place in refrigerator overnight.

- Preheat the grill.

- Arrange marinated pork chops on hot grill and cook for 3 minutes on each side.

- Serve and enjoy.

Per Serving: Net Carbs: 2g; Calories: 324; Total Fat: 26.5g; Saturated Fat: 8.4g
Protein: 18.4g; Carbs: 2.5g; Fiber: 0.5g; Sugar: 1.3g; Fat 74% / Protein 23% / Carbs 3%

Beef Kabobs

Serves: 8 / Preparation time: 10 minutes / Cooking time: 15 minutes

2 lbs top sirloin, cut into 1 ½- inch cubes

1 onion, cut into 1 ½-inch pieces

1 large zucchini, cut into ¼-inch slices

2 cups cherry tomatoes

2 bell peppers, sliced into 1 ½-inch pieces

For marinade:

¼ tsp cayenne pepper

1 tsp onion powder

1 tsp ground cumin

1 tsp ground coriander

2 tsp paprika

2 tsp garlic powder

1 tbsp dried oregano

2 tbsp balsamic vinegar

3 tbsp fresh lemon juice

¼ cup olive oil

¼ tsp pepper

1 tsp salt

- In a small bowl, whisk together all marinade ingredients.
- Add 2 tablespoons of marinade and vegetable in a medium bowl and mix well.
- In a separate bowl, mix together the remaining marinade and meat.
- Place vegetable and meat bowl in the refrigerator for overnight.
- Thread marinated vegetables and meat onto the skewers.
- Preheat the oven to 232 C/ 450 F.
- Line baking tray with foil and spray with cooking spray.
- Arrange kabobs on a baking tray and bake in preheated oven for 12-15 minutes or until cooked.
- Serve and enjoy.

Per Serving: Net Carbs: 6.3g; Calories: 352; Total Fat: 14.9g; Saturated Fat: 4.2g
Protein: 36.3g; Carbs: 8.6g; Fiber: 2.3g; Sugar: 4.8g; Fat 44% / Protein 46% / Carbs 10%

Classic Pork Chop Cacciatore

Serves: 6 / Preparation time: 10 minutes / Cooking time: 6 hours

1 ½ lbs pork chops

2 cups mushrooms, sliced

1 small onion, diced

1 garlic clove, minced

1 tsp dried oregano

1 cup beef broth

3 tbsp tomato paste

14 oz can tomatoes, diced

2 tbsp olive oil

¼ tsp pepper

½ tsp salt

- Heat oil in a pan over medium-high heat.
- Add pork chops in pan and cook until brown on both the sides.
- Transfer pork chops into the slow cooker.
- Pour remaining ingredients over the pork chops.
- Cover and cook on low for 6 hours.
- Serve and enjoy.

Per Serving: Net Carbs: 5.2g; Calories: 441 Total Fat: 33.2g; Saturated Fat: 11.3g
Protein: 28.2g; Carbs: 7.3g; Fiber: 2.1g; Sugar: 4.3g; Fat 68% / Protein 26% / Carbs 6%

Mediterranean Beef Kofta

Serves: 8 / Preparation time: 10 minutes / Cooking time: 10 minutes

2 lbs ground beef

2 tsp cumin

1 cup fresh parsley, chopped

4 garlic cloves, minced

1 onion, minced

¼ tsp pepper

1 tsp salt

- Add all ingredients into the mixing bowl and mix until combined.
- Shape meat mixture into the kabab shapes and cook in a hot pan for 4-6 minutes on each side or until cooked.
- Serve and enjoy.

Per Serving: Net Carbs: 1.8g; Calories: 223; Total Fat: 7.3g; Saturated Fat: 2.7g
Protein: 35g; Carbs: 2.5g; Fiber: 0.7g; Sugar: 0.7g; Fat 31% / Protein 64% / Carbs 5%

Lamb Meatballs

Serves: 4 / Preparation time: 10 minutes / Cooking time: 20 minutes

1 lb ground lamb

3 tbsp olive oil

¼ tsp red pepper flakes

1 tsp ground cumin

2 tsp fresh oregano, chopped

2 tbsp fresh parsley, chopped

1 tbsp garlic, minced

1 egg, lightly beaten

¼ tsp pepper

1 tsp kosher salt

- Preheat the oven to 218 C/ 425 F.
- Line baking tray with parchment paper.
- Add all ingredients except oil into the mixing bowl and mix until well combined.
- Make small meatballs from meat mixture and place on a prepared baking tray.
- Drizzle oil over meatballs and bake in preheated oven for 20 minutes.
- Serve and enjoy.

Per Serving: Net Carbs: 1.2g; Calories: 325; Total Fat: 20.2g; Saturated Fat: 4.8g
Protein: 33.6g; Carbs: 1.7g; Fiber: 0.5g; Sugar: 0.2g; Fat 56% / Protein 42% / Carbs 2%

Easy & Delicious Italian Pork Roast

Serves: 8 / Preparation time: 10 minutes / Cooking time: 6 hours

2 lbs lean pork roast, boneless

1 tsp dried oregano

1 tsp dried basil

1 tsp garlic powder

1 tbsp parsley

½ cup parmesan cheese, grated

28 oz can tomatoes, diced

Pepper

Salt

- Add the meat into the slow cooker.

- Mix together tomatoes, oregano, basil, garlic powder, parsley, cheese, pepper, and salt and pour over meat.

- Cover and cook on low for 6 hours.

- Serve and enjoy.

Per Serving: Net Carbs: 3.7g; Calories: 333 Total Fat: 15.2g; Saturated Fat: 6.9g
Protein: 39.3g; Carbs: 5.5g; Fiber: 1.8g; Sugar: 3.5g; Fat 44% / Protein 50% / Carbs 6%

Tender Lamb Roast

Serves: 8 / Preparation time: 10 minutes / Cooking time: 8 hours

4 lbs lamb roast, boneless

4 garlic cloves, cut into slivers

½ tsp marjoram

½ tsp thyme

1 tsp oregano

¼ tsp pepper

2 tsp salt

- Using a sharp knife make small cuts all over lamb roast then insert garlic slivers into the cuts.
- In a small bowl, mix together marjoram, thyme, oregano, pepper, and salt and rub all over lamb roast.
- Place lamb roast into the slow cooker.
- Cover and cook on low for 8 hours.
- Serve and enjoy.

Per Serving: Net Carbs: 0.5g; Calories: 605; Total Fat: 48.2g; Saturated Fat: 22.1g
Protein: 38.3g; Carbs: 0.7g; Fiber: 0.2g; Sugar: 0g; Fat 73% / Protein 26% / Carbs 1%

Beef Patties

Serves: 5 / Preparation time: 10 minutes / Cooking time: 8 minutes

1 lb ground beef

2 tbsp fresh parsley, chopped

1 tsp dry oregano

1 tsp dry mint

1 egg, lightly beaten

3 tbsp almond flour

1 small onion, grated

Pepper

Salt

- Add all ingredients into the mixing bowl and mix until combined.
- Make small patties from the meat mixture.
- Heat grill pan over medium-high heat.
- Place patties in a hot pan and cook for 4 minutes on each side.
- Serve and enjoy.

Per Serving: Net Carbs: 1.6g; Calories: 212; Total Fat: 8.7g; Saturated Fat: 2.6g
Protein: 29.8g; Carbs: 2.6g; Fiber: 1g; Sugar: 0.8g; Fat 39% / Protein 58% / Carbs 3%

Baked Lamb Patties

Serves: 4 / Preparation time: 10 minutes / Cooking time: 15 minutes

1 lb ground lamb

¼ tsp cayenne pepper

½ tsp ground allspice

1 tsp ground cinnamon

1 tsp ground coriander

1 tsp ground cumin

¼ cup fresh parsley, chopped

¼ cup onion, minced

1 tbsp garlic, minced

¼ tsp pepper

1 tsp kosher salt

- Preheat the oven to 232 C/ 450 F.
- Add all ingredients into the large bowl and mix until well combined.
- Make small balls from meat mixture and place on a baking tray and lightly flatten the meatballs with back on spoon.
- Bake in preheated oven for 12-15 minutes.
- Serve and enjoy.

Per Serving: Net Carbs: 1.8g; Calories: 223 Total Fat: 8.5g; Saturated Fat: 8.5g
Protein: 32.3g; Carbs: 2.6g; Fiber: 0.8g; Sugar: 0.4g; Fat 37% / Protein 59% / Carbs 4%

Italian Meatballs

Serves: 6 / Preparation time: 10 minutes / Cooking time: 4 hours

½ lb ground beef

½ lb ground pork

1 egg

2 tbsp fresh parsley, chopped

1 garlic clove, minced

14 oz can tomatoes, crushed

2 tbsp fresh basil, chopped

¼ tsp pepper

½ tsp salt

- In a mixing bowl, mix together beef, pork, egg, parsley, garlic, pepper, and salt until well combined.

- Make small balls from meat mixture.

- Arrange meatballs into the slow cooker.

- Pour crushed tomatoes, basil, pepper, and salt over meatballs.

- Cover and cook on low for 4 hours.

- Serve and enjoy.

Per Serving: Net Carbs: 2.6g; Calories: 150; Total Fat: 4.4g; Saturated Fat: 1.6g
Protein: 23g; Carbs: 3.8g; Fiber: 1.2g; Sugar: 2.3g; Fat 29% / Protein 63% / Carbs 8%

POULTRY RECIPES

Contents

Tomato Olive Chicken

Serves: 4 / Preparation time: 10 minutes / Cooking time: 22 minutes

4 chicken breast, boneless and halves

3 tbsp olive oil

3 tbsp capers, rinsed and drained

15 olives, pitted and halved

2 cups cherry tomatoes

Pepper

Salt

- Preheat the oven to 246 C/ 475 F.
- In a bowl, toss tomatoes, capers, olives with 2 tablespoons of olive oil. Set aside.
- Season chicken with pepper and salt.
- Heat remaining oil in a large pan over high heat.
- Place chicken in the pan and cook for 4 minutes. Turn chicken to the other side and top with tomato mixture.
- Transfer pan to oven and roast chicken in preheated oven for 18 minutes.
- Serve and enjoy.

Per Serving: Net Carbs: 3.1g; Calories: 404; Total Fat: 23.3g; Saturated Fat: 4.8g
Protein: 43.3g; Carbs: 4.9g; Fiber: 1.8g; Sugar: 2.4g; Fat 52% / Protein 44% / Carbs 4%

Healthy Chicken Salad

Serves: 4 / Preparation time: 10 minutes / Cooking time: 5 minutes

1 ½ cups chicken breast, skinless, boneless, and cooked

½ tsp onion powder

½ tbsp fresh lemon juice

1 tbsp fresh parsley, chopped

1 tbsp fresh dill, chopped

2 ½ tbsp mayonnaise

¼ cup Greek yogurt

2 tbsp onion, diced

¼ cup olives, diced

¼ cup roasted red peppers, diced

¼ cup cucumbers, diced

¼ cup celery, diced

¼ cup feta cheese, crumbled

¼ tsp pepper

½ tsp salt

- In a mixing bowl, mix together yogurt, onion powder, lemon juice, parsley, dill, mayonnaise, pepper, and salt.
- Add chicken, onion, olives, red peppers, cucumbers, and feta cheese and stir well.
- Serve and enjoy.

Per Serving: Net Carbs: 5.8g; Calories: 157 Total Fat: 8.9g; Saturated Fat: 2.9g
Protein: 12.4g; Carbs: 6.7g; Fiber: 0.9g; Sugar: 3.1g; Fat 53% / Protein 33% / Carbs 14%

Hearty Italian Chicken

Serves: 3 / Preparation time: 10 minutes / Cooking time: 15 minutes

½ lb chicken breast, skinless, boneless, and cut into cubes

¼ cup feta cheese, crumbled

¼ cup olives, sliced

½ tsp oregano

½ tsp basil

14 oz can tomatoes, diced

1 tsp garlic, minced

2 tbsp olive oil

Pepper

Salt

- Heat oil in a pan over medium heat.
- Season chicken with pepper and salt.
- Add chicken and cook for 5-7 minutes or until chicken is browned, Remove chicken from pan and set aside.
- Add tomatoes, olives, oregano, and basil to the pan and simmer over low heat for 7 minutes.
- Return chicken to the pan and stir well. Remove pan from heat.
- Sprinkle feta cheese on top of chicken mixture. Cover and let it sit for 5 minutes.
- Serve and enjoy.

Per Serving: Net Carbs: 5.1g; Calories: 238; Total Fat: 15.1g; Saturated Fat: 3.4g
Protein: 18.9 g; Carbs: 6.5g; Fiber: 1.4g; Sugar: 3.4g; Fat 59% / Protein 32% / Carbs 9%

Delicious Chicken Paillard

Serves: 8 / Preparation time: 10 minutes / Cooking time: 25 minutes

4 chicken breasts, skinless and boneless

¼ cup fresh basil, chopped

¼ cup fresh parsley, chopped

¼ cup pine nuts

½ cup olives, diced

1 small onion, sliced

1 fennel bulb, sliced

28 oz can tomatoes, diced

2 tbsp olive oil

Pepper

Salt

- Preheat the oven to 232 C/ 450 F.
- Arrange chicken in baking dish and season with pepper and salt and drizzle with oil.
- In a bowl, mix together olives, tomatoes, pine nuts, onion, fennel, pepper, and salt.
- Pour olive mixture over chicken and bake in preheated oven for 25 minutes.
- Garnish with basil and parsley.
- Serve and enjoy.

Per Serving: Net Carbs: 6g; Calories: 242; Total Fat: 12.8g; Saturated Fat: 2.3g
Protein: 23.2g; Carbs: 9.3g; Fiber: 3.3g; Sugar: 3.9g; Fat 49% / Protein 41% / Carbs 10%

Moist & Juicy Roasted Pepper Chicken

Serves: 4 / Preparation time: 10 minutes / Cooking time: 4 hours

2 lbs chicken breasts, skinless and boneless

½ cup feta cheese, crumbled

1 tsp dried thyme

1 tsp dried oregano

1 tbsp garlic, minced

3 tbsp red wine vinegar

1 onion, diced

½ cup olives

10 oz roasted red peppers, drained and chopped

1 tbsp olive oil

¼ tsp pepper

½ tsp kosher salt

- Spray slow cooker with cooking spray.

- Heat oil in a large pan over medium-high heat.

- Season chicken with pepper and salt and place in the hot pan and cook until brown from both the side. Transfer chicken to the slow cooker.

- Add onions, olives, and roasted red peppers around the chicken.

- In a small bowl, whisk together vinegar, thyme, oregano, and garlic and pour over chicken.

- Cover slow cooker and cook on low for 3-4 hours or until chicken is cooked through.

- Sprinkle crumbled cheese on top and serve.

Per Serving: Net Carbs: 4.6g; Calories: 551 Total Fat: 26.2g; Saturated Fat: 8.2g
Protein: 68.9g; Carbs: 6.1g; Fiber: 1.5g; Sugar: 2.3g; Fat 44% / Protein 53% / Carbs 3%

Chicken Green Bean Salad

Serves: 4 / Preparation time: 10 minutes / Cooking time: 5 minutes

4 chicken breasts, skinless, boneless, grilled, and cut into pieces

½ cup feta cheese, crumbled

½ lb green beans, cooked and cut into pieces

1 cup cherry tomatoes, halved

2 tbsp capers, drained

1 lemon juice

1 ½ tsp oregano

¼ cup olive oil

Pepper

Salt

- Add all ingredients into the large mixing bowl and toss well.
- Season salad with pepper and salt.
- Serve and enjoy.

Per Serving: Net Carbs: 4.5g; Calories: 466; Total Fat: 27.8g; Saturated Fat: 7.7g
Protein: 46.6g; Carbs: 7.4g; Fiber: 2.9g; Sugar: 3g; Fat 54% / Protein 42% / Carbs 4%

Chunky Chicken Salad

Serves: 4 / Preparation time: 10 minutes / Cooking time: 5 minutes

For salad:

4 cups cooked chicken breast, skinless, boneless, and shredded

5 garlic cloves, roasted and chopped

1/4 cup walnuts, chopped

1/2 cup parsley, chopped

1/4 cup sun-dried tomatoes

1/3 cup marinated artichoke hearts, chopped

2 celery stalks, chopped

1 small onion, chopped

For dressing:

1/2 tsp paprika

2 tsp Dijon mustard

1 tsp white wine vinegar

1 tsp lemon zest

1/3 cup olive oil

Pepper

Salt

- Add all salad ingredients into the large bowl and mix well.
- In a small bowl, whisk together all dressing ingredients and pour over salad and toss well.
- Serve and enjoy.

Per Serving: Net Carbs: 3.9g; Calories: 444; Total Fat: 27.4g; Saturated Fat: 4.1g
Protein: 43.6g; Carbs: 6g; Fiber: 2.1g; Sugar: 1.6g; Fat 56% / Protein 40% / Carbs 4%

Delicious & Creamy Chicken

Serves: 5 / Preparation time: 10 minutes / Cooking time: 15 minutes

1 ½ lbs chicken breasts, skinless and boneless

2 tbsp fresh basil, chopped

¼ cup feta cheese, crumbled

¼ cup parmesan cheese, grated

¼ cup sun-dried tomatoes, chopped

14 oz can artichoke hearts, drained and chopped

1 ¼ cup half and half

1 tsp garlic, minced

2 tbsp olive oil

Pepper

Salt

- Heat olive oil in a pan over medium heat.

- Season chicken with pepper and salt.

- Add chicken in the pan and cook for 4-5 minutes or until lightly brown. Turn chicken to other side and cook for 3-4 minutes more.

- Remove chicken from pan and place on a plate. Set aside.

- Add garlic to the pan and sauté for 30 seconds.

- Add olives, sun-dried tomatoes, artichoke, and half and half. Stir well and cook over low heat until slightly thicken.

- Return chicken to the pan along with parmesan cheese and stir well.

- Remove pan from heat.

- Garnish with basil and feta cheese and serve.

Per Serving: Net Carbs: 4.7g; Calories: 551 Total Fat: 31.5g; Saturated Fat: 13.8g
Protein: 53.3g; Carbs: 7.5g; Fiber: 2.8g; Sugar: 1.3g; Fat 54% / Protein 42% / Carbs 4%

Tasty Chicken Marinade

Serves: 4 / Preparation time: 10 minutes / Cooking time: 14 minutes

2 lbs chicken breasts, skinless and boneless

½ tsp onion powder

½ tsp red pepper flakes

1 tsp dried oregano

1 tbsp garlic, minced

3 tbsp olive oil

1 tbsp balsamic vinegar

2 tbsp fresh lemon juice

½ tsp pepper

½ tsp kosher salt

- Add all ingredients into the large zip-lock bag. Seal bag and shake well to coat. Place in refrigerator overnight.
- Heat grill over medium-high heat.
- Place marinated chicken on hot grill and cook for 5-7 minutes. Turn chicken to other side and cook for 5-7 minutes.
- Slice and serve.

Per Serving: Net Carbs: 1.3g; Calories: 530; Total Fat: 27.5g; Saturated Fat: 6.2g
Protein: 65.9g; Carbs: 1.7g; Fiber: 0.4g; Sugar: 0.4g; Fat 48% / Protein 51% / Carbs 1%

Greek Lemon Chicken

Serves: 4 / Preparation time: 10 minutes / Cooking time: 6 hours

4 chicken breasts, skinless and boneless

¼ cup fresh parsley, chopped

1 cup chicken stock

¾ tbsp lemon zest

¼ cup fresh lemon juice

2 tsp dried oregano

1 tbsp garlic, minced

1 tsp kosher salt

- Add all ingredients except parsley into the slow cooker and mix well.
- Cover and cook on low for 6 hours.
- Garnish with parsley and serve.

Per Serving: Net Carbs: 1.5g; Calories: 291; Total Fat: 11.2g; Saturated Fat: 3.2g
Protein: 42.9g; Carbs: 2.1g; Fiber: 0.6g; Sugar: 0.6g; Fat 37% / Protein 61% / Carbs 2%

Tender & Juicy Garlic Chicken

Serves: 6 / Preparation time: 10 minutes / Cooking time: 40 minutes

2 lbs chicken thighs, skinless and boneless

2 tbsp fresh parsley, chopped

1 fresh lemon juice

8 garlic cloves, sliced

2 tbsp olive oil

Pepper

Salt

- Preheat the oven to 232 C/ 450 F.
- Place chicken on baking tray and season with pepper and salt.
- Sprinkle parsley and garlic over the chicken and drizzle oil and lemon juice on top of chicken.
- Bake in preheated oven for 30-40 minutes.
- Serve and enjoy.

Per Serving: Net Carbs: 1.4g; Calories: 336 Total Fat: 16g; Saturated Fat: 3.8g
Protein: 44.1g; Carbs: 1.6g; Fiber: 0.2g; Sugar: 0.2g; Fat 44% / Protein 54% / Carbs 2%

Grilled Chicken

Serves: 8 / Preparation time: 10 minutes / Cooking time: 12 minutes

8 chicken thighs, skinless and boneless

1 lemon juice

1 medium onion, sliced

¼ cup olive oil

¼ tsp cardamom powder

½ tsp ground nutmeg

½ tsp allspice

½ tsp paprika

8 garlic cloves, minced

Pepper

Salt

- In a small bowl, mix together 3 tablespoons of olive oil, garlic, and spices and rub over chicken.
- Add sliced onion, remaining oil, and lemon juice in the large dish then place chicken on top of sliced onion. Cover and place in the refrigerator overnight.
- Heat grill to medium-high heat. Place marinated chicken on the hot grill and cook for 5-6 minutes, then turn and cook for 5-6 minutes more.
- Serve and enjoy.

Per Serving: Net Carbs: 2.2g; Calories: 344; Total Fat: 17.3g; Saturated Fat: 4g
Protein: 42.7g; Carbs: 2.7g; Fiber: 0.5g; Sugar: 0.8g; Fat 47% / Protein 51% / Carbs 2%

Lemon Butter Chicken

Serves: 4 / Preparation time: 10 minutes / Cooking time: 20 minutes

4 chicken breasts, skinless and boneless

1/3 cup feta cheese, crumbled

¼ cup butter

2 tbsp fresh chives, chopped

2 tbsp fresh oregano, chopped

1 lemon juice

1 tsp lemon zest

2 tbsp capers

1/3 cup sun-dried olives

½ cup dry white wine

½ cup chicken stock

1 cup mushrooms, sliced

3 tbsp olive oil

1 tsp garlic, minced

Pepper

Salt

- Season chicken with pepper and salt.

- Heat olive oil in a pan over medium-high heat.

- Add chicken to the pan and cook for 4 minutes on each side or until chicken is cooked. Remove chicken from pan and set aside.

- Add garlic in the same pan and sauté for 30 seconds.

- Add mushrooms, white wine, and stock and simmer until liquid reduces by half.

- Return chicken to the pan along with remaining ingredients except for crumbled feta cheese.

- Cook chicken until butter is melted.

- Top with feta cheese and serve.

Per Serving: Net Carbs: 4.9g; Calories: 594; Total Fat: 41g; Saturated Fat: 13.8g
Protein: 45.3g; Carbs: 6.3g; Fiber: 1.4g; Sugar: 1.6g; Fat 64% / Protein 32% / Carbs 4%

Bacon Chicken Salad

Serves: 8 / Preparation time: 10 minutes / Cooking time: 5 minutes

2 lbs rotisserie chicken, shredded

¼ tsp garlic powder

¼ tsp onion powder

2/3 cup mayonnaise

1 avocado, diced

1 cup cherry tomatoes, quartered

4 bacon slices, cooked and chopped

Pepper

Salt

- Add chicken, avocado, bacon, and tomatoes into the mixing bowl and mix well.
- Mix together mayonnaise, garlic powder, onion powder, pepper, and salt and pour over chicken mixture. Stir until well combined.
- Serve and enjoy.

Per Serving: Net Carbs: 5.7g; Calories: 287 Total Fat: 15.4g; Saturated Fat: 3g
Protein: 31.7g; Carbs: 6.4g; Fiber: 0.7g; Sugar: 1.9g; Fat 48% / Protein 44% / Carbs 8%

Flavorful Chicken Shawarma

Serves: 5 / Preparation time: 10 minutes / Cooking time: 3 hours

1 ¼ lbs chicken thigh, skinless and boneless

¼ tsp ground coriander

¼ tsp cinnamon

½ tsp curry powder

½ tsp dried parsley

1 tsp paprika

1 tsp garlic powder

1 tsp cumin

2 tbsp garlic, minced

½ cup Greek yogurt

¼ cup chicken stock

¼ cup fresh lemon juice

1 ½ tbsp tahini

1 tbsp olive oil

Pepper

Salt

- Add chicken into the slow cooker and season with pepper and salt.
- Pour remaining ingredients over chicken.
- Cover and cook on high for 3 hours.
- Stir well and serve.

Per Serving: Net Carbs: 4.3g; Calories: 314; Total Fat: 14.8g; Saturated Fat: 3.9g
Protein: 38.8g; Carbs: 5.2g; Fiber: 0.9g; Sugar: 2.4g; Fat 44% / Protein 51% / Carbs 5%

Chicken Avocado Salad

Serves: 4 / Preparation time: 10 minutes / Cooking time: 5 minutes

2 cups chicken breast, cooked and chopped

¼ tsp red chili flakes

¼ tsp cumin

2 tbsp onion, chopped

2 tbsp fresh parsley, chopped

2 tbsp fresh lime juice

1 avocado

Pepper

Salt

- Add avocado into the bowl and mash using the fork.
- Add remaining ingredients and stir to combine.
- Serve and enjoy.

Per Serving: Net Carbs: 1.5g; Calories: 175; Total Fat: 12.6g; Saturated Fat: 2.8g
Protein: 11.5g; Carbs: 5.1g; Fiber: 3.6g; Sugar: 0.5g; Fat 67% / Protein 29% / Carbs 4%

Chicken Olive Salad

Serves: 4 / Preparation time: 10 minutes / Cooking time: 5 minutes

1 lb chicken breasts, skinless, boneless, cooked, and shredded

2 tbsp fresh parsley, chopped

1 tbsp fresh basil, chopped

1 tbsp fresh oregano, chopped

¼ tsp chili flakes

¾ cup olives, pitted and sliced

1 tbsp capers

2 tbsp olive oil

2 tbsp red wine vinegar

½ cup onion, minced

Pepper

Salt

- Add all ingredients into the large mixing bowl and toss well.
- Serve and enjoy.

Per Serving: Net Carbs: 2.2g; Calories: 317 Total Fat: 18.3g; Saturated Fat: 3.7g
Protein: 33.4g; Carbs: 4g; Fiber: 1.8g; Sugar: 0.7g; Fat 53% / Protein 44% / Carbs 3%

Creamy Greek Chicken Salad

Serves: 4 / Preparation time: 10 minutes / Cooking time: 5 minutes

2 cups chicken breast, skinless, boneless, cooked, and chopped

1 tsp garlic, minced

1 medium cucumber, chopped

2 tbsp fresh dill, chopped

1 tbsp fresh lemon juice

1/3 cup onion, chopped

2/3 cup Greek yogurt

Pepper

Salt

- Add all ingredients into the mixing bowl and mix until well combined.
- Place salad bowl in the refrigerator for 30 minutes before serving.
- Serve and enjoy.

Per Serving: Net Carbs: 6.3g; Calories: 163 Total Fat: 8.7g; Saturated Fat: 4.6g
Protein: 13.6g; Carbs: 7g; Fiber: 0.7g; Sugar: 4.1g; Fat 50% / Protein 35% / Carbs 15%

Creamy Roasted Pepper Chicken

Serves: 6 / Preparation time: 10 minutes / Cooking time: 20 minutes

2 lbs chicken breasts, skinless, boneless, and chopped

2 oz feta cheese, crumbled

1 cup heavy cream

5 tbsp olive oil

5 garlic cloves

1 cup roasted red peppers

1 tsp oregano

1 tsp basil

¼ tsp pepper

½ tsp salt

- Heat 1 tablespoon of oil in a pan over medium heat.

- Add chicken and season with basil and oregano and cook until chicken is browned.

- Add garlic, remaining oil, roasted red peppers, pepper, and salt into the blender and blend until smooth.

- Transfer chicken to a plate and set aside.

- Pour blended mixture into the pan and cook for 1-2 minutes.

- Add heavy cream and cook until heat through.

- Return chicken to pan and stir well.

- Remove pan from heat. Sprinkle with crumbled feta cheese and serve.

Per Serving: Net Carbs: 3g; Calories: 492; Total Fat: 32.4g; Saturated Fat: 10.8g
Protein: 45.9g; Carbs: 3.5g; Fiber: 0.5g; Sugar: 1.8g; Fat 60% / Protein 38% / Carbs 2%

Chicken Artichoke Hearts

Serves: 6 / Preparation time: 10 minutes / Cooking time: 8 hours

6 chicken thighs, skinless and boneless

1 tsp dried oregano

15 olives, pitted

3 tbsp fresh lemon juice

10 oz frozen artichoke hearts

14 oz can tomatoes, diced

½ tsp garlic powder

1 tsp dried basil

Pepper

Salt

- Spray slow cooker with cooking spray.
- Season chicken with pepper and salt and place in the slow cooker.
- Pour remaining ingredients over chicken.
- Cover and cook on low for 6-8 hours.
- Serve and enjoy.

Per Serving: Net Carbs: 5.3g; Calories: 182 Total Fat: 8.3g; Saturated Fat: 0.3g
Protein: 21.4g; Carbs: 9.5g; Fiber: 4.2g; Sugar: 3g; Fat 42% / Protein 47% / Carbs 11%

SEAFOOD RECIPES

Contents

Roasted Salmon

Serves: 4 / Preparation time: 10 minutes / Cooking time: 15 minutes

4 salmon fillets

2 tomatoes, sliced

1 small onion, sliced

1 tsp dried oregano

1 tsp dried rosemary

1 tsp dried thyme

2 tbsp fresh lemon juice

2 tbsp Dijon mustard

¼ tsp pepper

½ tsp salt

- In a shallow dish, mix together lemon juice, oregano, rosemary, thyme, mustard, pepper, and salt.

- Add fish fillets and coat well form both sides. Cover and place in the refrigerator for 15 minutes.

- Preheat the oven to 232 C/ 450 F.

- Spray a shallow baking dish with cooking spray.

- Arrange sliced tomatoes and onion in the bottom of a prepared baking dish then place marinated fish fillets on top. Pour remaining marinade over fish fillets.

- Roast in preheated oven for 10-15 minutes.

- Serve and enjoy.

Per Serving: Net Carbs: 3.5g; Calories: 264; Total Fat: 11.6g; Saturated Fat: 1.7g
Protein: 35.7g; Carbs: 5.3g; Fiber: 1.8g; Sugar: 2.6g; Fat 40% / Protein 54% / Carbs 6%

Seafood Salad

Serves: 4 / Preparation time: 10 minutes / Cooking time: 10 minutes

½ lb cooked shrimp

¼ tsp red pepper flakes

1 tbsp olive oil

3 tbsp fresh lemon juice

2 tbsp roasted red pepper, chopped

½ cup celery, chopped

1 cup crab meat

1/2 cup cooked calamari

½ tsp sea salt

- Add all ingredients into the mixing bowl and toss well.
- Cover and place in the refrigerator for 10 hours.
- Serve and enjoy.

Per Serving: Net Carbs: 6.6g; Calories: 231; Total Fat: 7.7g; Saturated Fat: 1.4g
Protein: 31g; Carbs: 7.2g; Fiber: 0.6g; Sugar: 0.7g; Fat 33% / Protein 55% / Carbs 12%

Roasted Salmon

Serves: 6 / Preparation time: 10 minutes / Cooking time: 40 minutes

2 lbs salmon fillet, skinless

¾ cup olive oil

4 dill sprigs

1 jalapeno pepper, sliced

1 lemon, sliced

1 orange, sliced

1 fennel bulb, sliced

Pepper

Salt

- Preheat the oven to 135 C/ 275 F.
- Toss dill, jalapeno, lemon slices, orange slices, fennel in baking dish.
- Season salmon with pepper and salt and place on top of dill mixture in baking dish.
- Pour oil over salmon and roast in preheated oven for 30-40 minutes.
- Transfer salmon to a plate and cut salmon into large pieces and serve.

Per Serving: Net Carbs: 5.2g; Calories: 446 Total Fat: 34.7g; Saturated Fat: 4.9g
Protein: 30.2g; Carbs: 7.5g; Fiber: 2.3g; Sugar: 3.2g; Fat 71% / Protein 28% / Carbs 1%

Buttery Shrimp

Serves: 4 / Preparation time: 10 minutes / Cooking time: 5 minutes

1 lb shrimp, deveined

1 lemon juice

½ tsp paprika

1 tsp Italian seasoning

1 tsp garlic, minced

1 stick butter

¼ tsp pepper

½ tsp salt

- Melt butter in a pan over medium heat.
- Add garlic and sauté for 30 seconds.
- Toss shrimp with paprika, Italian seasoning, pepper, and salt and add in the pan and cook for 2-3 minutes per side.
- Drizzle with lemon juice and serve.

Per Serving: Net Carbs: 2.4g; Calories: 346; Total Fat: 25.3g; Saturated Fat: 15.3g
Protein: 26.3g; Carbs: 2.6g; Fiber: 0.2g; Sugar: 0.4g; Fat 66% / Protein 31% / Carbs 3%

Baked Shrimp

Serves: 4 / Preparation time: 10 minutes / Cooking time: 13 minutes

1 ¼ lbs shrimp, peeled and deveined

2 tbsp fresh parsley, minced

1/8 tsp red pepper flakes

2 tbsp fresh lemon juice

1 tbsp garlic, minced

¼ cup butter

Pepper

Salt

- Preheat the oven to 350 F/ 180 C.
- Add shrimp in baking dish.
- Melt butter in a pan over low heat. Add garlic and sauté for 30 seconds.
- Remove melted butter from heat. Add lemon juice and stir well.
- Pour butter mixture over shrimp in the baking dish and season shrimp with red pepper flakes, pepper, and salt.
- Bake in preheated oven for 10-13 minutes.
- Garnish with parsley and serve.

Per Serving: Net Carbs: 3.0g; Calories: 276; Total Fat: 14g; Saturated Fat: 8.1g
Protein: 32.7g; Carbs: 3.2g; Fiber: 0.2g; Sugar: 0.2g; Fat 47% / Protein 49% / Carbs 4%

Shrimp Artichoke Salad

Serves: 8 / Preparation time: 10 minutes / Cooking time: 10 minutes

1 ½ lbs shrimp, cooked

1/3 cup feta cheese, crumbled

1 tbsp fresh parsley, chopped

¼ cup onion, chopped

¼ cup roasted red pepper, chopped

1 cup cherry tomatoes, halved

6 oz can olives

14 oz can artichoke hearts, drained and quartered

3 tbsp olive oil

¼ cup balsamic vinegar

1 tbsp Italian seasoning

Pepper

Salt

- In a small bowl, whisk together Italian seasoning, vinegar, and oil. Set aside.
- Add remaining ingredients into the mixing bowl and mix well.
- Pour dressing over salad and toss well.
- Serve and enjoy.

Per Serving: Net Carbs: 4.4g; Calories: 216 Total Fat: 10.9g; Saturated Fat: 2.5g
Protein: 21.6g; Carbs: 7.2g; Fiber: 2.8g; Sugar: 1.8g; Fat 48% / Protein 43% / Carbs 9%

Salmon Patties

Serves: 4 / Preparation time: 10 minutes / Cooking time: 20 minutes

14 oz can salmon, drained and flaked with a fork

¼ cup almond flour

½ cup fresh parsley, chopped

1 tsp Dijon mustard

1 tbsp garlic, minced

2 eggs, lightly beaten

¼ tsp pepper

½ tsp kosher salt

- Preheat the oven to 400 F/ 200 C.
- Spray a baking tray with cooking spray and set aside.
- Add all ingredients into the mixing bowl and mix until well combined.
- Make small patties and place on a prepared baking tray.
- Bake in preheated oven for 10 minutes. Turn patties and bake for 10 minutes more.
- Serve and enjoy.

Per Serving: Net Carbs: 1.9g; Calories: 216; Total Fat: 11.8g; Saturated Fat: 2.5g
Protein: 24.3g; Carbs: 3g; Fiber: 1.1g; Sugar: 0.5g; Fat 51% / Protein 46% / Carbs 3%

Rosemary Salmon

Serves: 4 / Preparation time: 10 minutes / Cooking time: 15 minutes

1 lbs salmon, cut into 4 pieces

1/4 tsp dried basil

1 tbsp dried chives

1 tbsp olive oil

1/2 tbsp dried rosemary

Pepper

Salt

- Place salmon pieces skin side down into the air fryer basket.
- Mix together olive oil, basil, chives, and rosemary. Brush salmon with oil mixture.
- Air fry at 400 F/ 200 C for 15 minutes.
- Serve and enjoy.

Per Serving: Net Carbs: 0.1g; Calories: 182; Total Fat: 10.6g; Saturated Fat: 1.5g
Protein: 22g; Carbs: 0.3g; Fiber: 0.2g; Sugar: 0g; Fat 51% / Protein 48% / Carbs 1%

Greek Tuna Patties

14 oz can tuna

3 tbsp olive oil

½ tsp lemon zest

1 tsp dried oregano

2 tbsp fresh mint, chopped

1 tbsp lemon juice

2 tbsp green onions, minced

3 tbsp flax meal

½ cup feta cheese, crumbled

1 egg, lightly beaten

1 garlic clove, minced

Pepper

Salt

- Add all ingredients except olive oil into the large bowl and mix until well combined.
- Heat oil in a pan over medium heat.
- Make small patties from tuna mixture and place on a hot pan.
- Cook tuna patties for 5-6 minutes. Turn and cook for 3 minutes more.
- Serve and enjoy.

Per Serving: Net Carbs: 1g; Calories: 199 Total Fat: 12.2g; Saturated Fat: 3.3g
Protein: 20.5g; Carbs: 2.3g; Fiber: 1.3g; Sugar: 0.7g; Fat 56% / Protein 42% / Carbs 2%

Spanish Shrimp

Serves: 4 / Preparation time: 10 minutes / Cooking time: 6 minutes

1 lb shrimp, peeled and deveined

2 tbsp fresh parsley, chopped

2 tbsp fresh lemon juice

1 ½ tbsp dry sherry

1 tsp Spanish paprika

¼ tsp chili flakes

1 tbsp garlic, chopped

1/3 cup olive oil

1/8 tsp pepper

¼ tsp kosher salt

- Add oil into the pan and heat over medium-high heat.

- Add chili flakes and garlic and sauté for 1 minute.

- Add shrimp and season with paprika, pepper, and salt and sauté for 2 minutes or until shrimp turns to pink in color.

- Add lemon juice and sherry and cook for 2-3 minutes.

- Garnish with parsley and serve.

Per Serving: Net Carbs: 3.5g; Calories: 294; Total Fat: 19.1g; Saturated Fat: 3.1g
Protein: 26.3g; Carbs: 3.9g; Fiber: 0.4g; Sugar: 0.2g; Fat 59% / Protein 36% / Carbs 5%

Tuna Cakes

Serves: 4 / Preparation time: 10 minutes / Cooking time: 10 minutes

14 oz can tuna, drained

2 tbsp olive oil

½ tsp ground cumin

½ tsp garlic powder

½ lemon juice

1 jalapeno pepper, diced

¼ cup almond flour

¼ cup yogurt

½ cup fresh cilantro, minced

1 egg, lightly beaten

Pepper

Salt

- Add all ingredients except oil into the large bowl and mix until well combined.
- Heat oil in a pan over medium heat.
- Make small patties from tuna mixture and place on a hot pan and cook for 5 minutes.
- Turn patties and cook for 5 minutes more.
- Serve and enjoy.

Per Serving: Net Carbs: 2.5g; Calories: 247; Total Fat: 12.7g; Saturated Fat: 2g
Protein: 29.3g; Carbs: 3.5g; Fiber: 1g; Sugar: 1.8g; Fat 47% / Protein 48% / Carbs 5%

Roasted Red Snapper

Serves: 2 / Preparation time: 10 minutes / Cooking time: 15 minutes

1 lb red snapper fillet

¾ cup white wine

2 fresh rosemary sprigs

¼ tsp herb de Provence

1 garlic clove, crushed

2 tbsp olive oil

Pepper

Salt

- Preheat the oven to 400 F/ 200 C.
- Line baking tray with foil.
- Season fish fillet with pepper and salt and place on a baking tray.
- Drizzle oil over fish. Place rosemary, garlic, and herb de Provence on top of fish.
- Roast fish in preheated oven for 10 minutes.
- Slowly pour wine over fish fillet and continue roast for 5 minutes.
- Serve hot and enjoy.

Per Serving: Net Carbs: 2.9g; Calories: 486 Total Fat: 17.9g; Saturated Fat: 2.8g
Protein: 59.8g; Carbs: 2.9g; Fiber: 0g; Sugar: 0.7g; Fat 40% / Protein 56% / Carbs 4%

Fish Stew

Serves: 3 / Preparation time: 10 minutes / Cooking time: 35 minutes

4 cod fillets

1/8 tsp cayenne

½ tsp paprika

¼ cup olive oil

1 cup of water

1 ½ cups onion, sliced

¼ tsp pepper

1 tsp salt

- Add oil, cayenne, paprika, onion, water, pepper, and salt into the pan and bring to boil over medium-high heat.

- Turn heat to low and simmer for 10-15 minutes or until onion is softened.

- Add fish fillets and cook for 10-15 minutes or until fish is cooked.

- Serve and enjoy.

Per Serving: Net Carbs: 4.3g; Calories: 289; Total Fat: 18.3g; Saturated Fat: 2.4g
Protein: 27.4g; Carbs: 5.7g; Fiber: 1.4g; Sugar: 2.5g; Fat 57% / Protein 38% / Carbs 5%

Cod Salad

Serves: 3 / Preparation time: 10 minutes / Cooking time: 5 minutes

12 oz cod fillet, soak for 12 hours

1 garlic clove, minced

1 tbsp olive oil

1 tbsp parsley, chopped

- Cook cod for 4-5 minutes or until cooked.
- Cut cooked cod into the pieces and place them on a plate.
- Drizzle oil over cod and sprinkle with garlic and parsley.
- Serve and enjoy.

Per Serving: Net Carbs: 0.3g; Calories: 161; Total Fat: 5.7g; Saturated Fat: 0.9g
Protein: 26g; Carbs: 0.4g; Fiber: 0.1 g; Sugar: 0g; Fat 33% / Protein 66% / Carbs 1%

Lemon Garlic Tilapia

Serves: 6 / Preparation time: 10 minutes / Cooking time: 12 minutes

1 lb tilapia fillets, cut into 2-inch pieces

3 tbsp fresh parsley, chopped

2 tsp dried oregano

4 garlic cloves, minced

¼ cup fresh lemon juice

5 tbsp butter

Pepper

Salt

- Melt butter in a pan over medium heat.

- Add lemon juice and stir well.

- Add fish pieces into the pan and sprinkle with parsley, oregano, garlic, pepper, and salt and cook for 6 minutes.

- Turn fish pieces and cook for 6 minutes more.

- Serve and enjoy.

Per Serving: Net Carbs: 0.9g; Calories: 155 Total Fat: 10.4g; Saturated Fat: 6.5g
Protein: 14.5g; Carbs: 1.3g; Fiber: 0.4g; Sugar: 0.3g; Fat 61% / Protein 37% / Carbs 2%

Baked White Fish

Serves: 1 / Preparation time: 10 minutes / Cooking time: 30 minutes

8 oz frozen white fish fillet

1 tbsp fresh parsley, chopped

1 tbsp roasted red bell pepper, diced

½ tsp Italian seasoning

1 ½ tbsp butter, melted

1 tbsp lemon juice

- Preheat the oven to 400 F/ 200 C.

- Line baking tray with foil and place fish fillet on a baking tray.

- Drizzle butter and lemon juice over fish. Sprinkle with Italian seasoning.

- Top with roasted bell pepper and parsley and bake in preheated oven for 30 minutes.

- Serve and enjoy.

Per Serving: Net Carbs: 1g; Calories: 357; Total Fat: 18.8g; Saturated Fat: 11.4g
Protein: 46.8g; Carbs: 1.3g; Fiber: 0.3g; Sugar: 0.8g; Fat 47% / Protein 52% / Carbs 1%

Salmon Salad

Serves: 2 / Preparation time: 10 minutes / Cooking time: 16 minutes

10 oz salmon fillet

¼ cup fennel, chopped

½ cucumber, chopped

1 tomato, chopped

1 lemon juice

1 tbsp olive oil

Pepper

Salt

For dressing:

1 tbsp fresh dill, chopped

1 tbsp lemon juice

1 tbsp balsamic vinegar

¼ cup olive oil

- Heat grill over medium-high heat.

- In a bowl, add salmon, 1 tbsp oil, 1 lemon juice, pepper, and salt and coat well.

- Place marinated salmon on hot grill and cook for 6-8 minutes from both sides.

- Shred salmon using fork and place in a large bowl. Add tomato, cucumber, and fennel and mix well.

- In a small bowl, whisk together all dressing ingredients and pour over salmon mixture and toss well.

- Serve and enjoy.

Per Serving: Net Carbs: 5g; Calories: 497; Total Fat: 41.4g; Saturated Fat: 6.1g
Protein: 29g; Carbs: 6.4g; Fiber: 1.4g; Sugar: 2.8g; Fat 73% / Protein 23% / Carbs 4%

Haddock Salad

Serves: 6 / Preparation time: 10 minutes / Cooking time: 5 minutes

1 lb haddock, cooked

1 tbsp olive oil

1 tsp garlic, minced

1 tbsp green onion, chopped

Pepper

Salt

- Flake the cooked haddock and place it on a plate.
- Drizzle with oil and season with pepper and salt.
- Sprinkle garlic and green onion over haddock.
- Serve and enjoy.

Per Serving: Net Carbs: 0.1g; Calories: 106 Total Fat: 3g; Saturated Fat: 0.5g
Protein: 18.4g; Carbs: 0.2g; Fiber: 0.1g; Sugar: 0g; Fat 27% / Protein 71% / Carbs 2%

Greek Style Salmon

Serves: 4 / Preparation time: 10 minutes / Cooking time: 10 minutes

24 oz salmon, cut into 4 pieces

1 tsp oregano

1 garlic clove, grated

1 tbsp yogurt

1 tsp lemon zest

2 tbsp lemon juice

2 tbsp olive oil

¼ tsp pepper

¼ tsp salt

- Add all ingredients except salmon in a baking dish and mix well.
- Add salmon and coat well and let it sit for 30 minutes.
- Preheat the oven to 400 F/ 200 C.
- Place baking dish in preheated oven and bake salmon for 10 minutes.
- Serve and enjoy.

Per Serving: Net Carbs: 0.8g; Calories: 292; Total Fat: 17.7g; Saturated Fat: 2.6g
Protein: 33.4g; Carbs: 1.1g; Fiber: 0.3g; Sugar: 0.5g; Fat 54% / Protein 45% / Carbs 1%

Lemon Oregano Shrimp

Serves: 3 / Preparation time: 10 minutes / Cooking time: 8 minutes

1 lb shrimp, shell removed

1 tbsp oregano

¼ cup olive oil

1 lemon juice

¼ tsp red pepper flakes

Pepper

Salt

- Add shrimp into the mixing bowl.
- Add remaining ingredients over shrimp and toss well and place in the refrigerator for 1 hour.
- Preheat the grill.
- Thread marinated shrimp onto the skewers.
- Arrange shrimp skewers on hot grill and cook for 4 minutes on each side or until cooked.
- Serve and enjoy.

Per Serving: Net Carbs: 2.9g; Calories: 333; Total Fat: 19.7g; Saturated Fat: 3.4g
Protein: 34.8g; Carbs: 3.7g; Fiber: 0.8g; Sugar: 0.4g; Fat 54% / Protein 42% / Carbs 4%

Grilled Scallops

Serves: 6 / Preparation time: 10 minutes / Cooking time: 4 minutes

1 lb scallops

1 tbsp Italian seasoning

1 tsp garlic, minced

1 lemon juice

¼ cup olive oil

Pepper

Salt

- In a bowl, mix together oil, Italian seasoning, garlic, and lemon juice.

- Season scallops with pepper and salt and add in the bowl and toss until well coated. Cover bowl and place in the refrigerator for 30 minutes.

- Preheat the grill over medium-high heat.

- Arrange marinated scallops on grill and cook for 2 minutes on each side.

- Serve and enjoy.

Per Serving: Net Carbs: 2.3g; Calories: 148 Total Fat: 9.7g; Saturated Fat: 1.4g
Protein: 12.8g; Carbs: 2.4g; Fiber: 0.1g; Sugar: 0.4g; Fat 59% / Protein 35% / Carbs 6%

Protein Packed Shrimp Salad

Serves: 6 / Preparation time: 10 minutes / Cooking time: 5 minutes

2 lbs shrimp, cooked

¼ tsp cayenne pepper

1 tbsp fresh lemon juice

1 tbsp olive oil

¼ cup mayonnaise

¼ cup onion, minced

¼ cup fresh dill, chopped

1/3 cup fresh chives, chopped

½ cup fresh celery, chopped

¼ tsp pepper

¼ tsp salt

- In a large mixing bowl, add all ingredients except shrimp and mix well.
- Add shrimp and toss well.
- Serve and enjoy.

Per Serving: Net Carbs: 6.1g; Calories: 248; Total Fat: 8.3g; Saturated Fat: 1.6g
Protein: 35.2g; Carbs: 6.7g; Fiber: 0.6g; Sugar: 1.1g; Fat 32% / Protein 58% / Carbs 10%

Poached Cod

Serves: 4 / Preparation time: 10 minutes / Cooking time: 5 minutes

1 lb fresh cod

½ cup olives, chopped

2 tbsp capers

2 cups baby spinach

3 tbsp tomato paste

1 cup vegetable broth

1 cup white wine

1 tsp garlic, sliced

¾ cup cherry tomatoes, halved

½ onion, sliced

1 tbsp olive oil

Pepper

Salt

- Heat oil in a large pan over medium heat.
- Add garlic, onion, and tomatoes and cook for 5 minutes.
- Add wine and simmer for 5 minutes.
- Add spinach, olives, capers, tomato paste, and broth and simmer over low heat for 15-20 minutes.
- Add cod and stir well. Cover and cook over medium heat for 6-10 minutes.
- Serve and enjoy.

Per Serving: Net Carbs: 6.5g; Calories: 254; Total Fat: 6.9g; Saturated Fat: 1.1g
Protein: 28.8g; Carbs: 8.7g; Fiber: 2.2g; Sugar: 3.7g; Fat 34% / Protein 55% / Carbs 11%

Braised Cod

Serves: 6 / Preparation time: 10 minutes / Cooking time: 15 minutes

1 ½ lbs cod fillets

½ cup olives, chopped

28 oz can tomatoes, diced

½ cup dry white wine

½ tsp red pepper flakes

½ tsp fennel seeds, crushed

1 tsp dried oregano

1 tbsp garlic, minced

1 tbsp olive oil

- Heat oil in a large pan over medium heat.
- Add garlic and sauté for 30 seconds.
- Add fennel, oregano, and red pepper flakes and sauté for 30 seconds.
- Add white wine and simmer over medium-high heat until the liquid reduces by half.
- Add olives and tomatoes and simmer for 5 minutes.
- Add cod fillets and stir well. Cover and cook for 5 minutes or until fish is tender.
- Serve and enjoy.

Per Serving: Net Carbs: 5.9g; Calories: 200 Total Fat: 4.6g; Saturated Fat: 0.7g
Protein: 27.4g; Carbs: 8.8g; Fiber: 2.9g; Sugar: 4.7g; Fat 26% / Protein 60% / Carbs 14%

Crab Salad

Serves: 6 / Preparation time: 10 minutes / Cooking time: 5 minutes

1 lb lump crabmeat

½ tsp Dijon mustard

1 tsp fresh lemon juice

3 tbsp sour cream

1/3 cup mayonnaise

1 tsp tarragon, minced

4 tsp fresh chives, sliced

1 celery stalk, diced

Pepper

Salt

- In a mixing bowl, toss together crabmeat, tarragon, chives, and celery.
- In a small bowl, whisk together mayonnaise, mustard, lemon juice, and sour cream and pour over crabmeat mixture and stir well.
- Season salad with pepper and salt.
- Serve and enjoy.

Per Serving: Net Carbs: 3.5g; Calories: 142; Total Fat: 7g; Saturated Fat: 1.6g
Protein: 15.7g; Carbs: 3.6g; Fiber: 0.1g; Sugar: 0.9g; Fat 46% / Protein 46% / Carbs 8%

Flavorful Baked Salmon

Serves: 5 / Preparation time: 10 minutes / Cooking time: 20 minutes

1 ¾ lbs salmon fillet

1/3 cup basil pesto

1 tbsp fresh dill, chopped

¼ cup capers

1/3 cup artichoke hearts

¼ cup sun-dried tomatoes, drained

¼ cup olives, pitted and chopped

1 tsp paprika

¼ tsp salt

- Preheat the oven to 400 F/ 200 C.
- Line baking tray with parchment paper.
- Arrange salmon fillet on a prepared baking tray and sprinkle with paprika and salt.
- Add remaining ingredients on top of salmon and spread evenly.
- Bake in preheated oven for 20 minutes.
- Serve and enjoy.

Per Serving: Net Carbs: 2.4g; Calories: 285; Total Fat: 13.4g; Saturated Fat: 1.9g
Protein: 39.5g; Carbs: 3.4g; Fiber: 1g; Sugar: 0.4g; Fat 42% / Protein 55% / Carbs 3%

Greek Tilapia

Serves: 2 / Preparation time: 10 minutes / Cooking time: 17 minutes

½ lb tilapia fillets, remove bones

2 oz feta cheese, crumbled

2/3 cup tomatoes, chopped

1/3 cup fresh parsley, chopped

1 tsp olive oil

1 ½ tbsp garlic, minced

Pepper

Salt

- Preheat the oven to 400 F/ 200 C.
- In a medium bowl, mix together tomatoes, garlic, feta, parsley, and olive oil.
- Spray tilapia fillets with cooking spray and season with pepper and salt.
- Place tilapia fillets on baking tray and top and with tomato mixture.
- Bake in preheated oven for 15-17 minutes.
- Serve and enjoy.

Per Serving: Net Carbs: 5g; Calories: 212 Total Fat: 9.6g; Saturated Fat: 5.1g
Protein: 26.4g; Carbs: 6.2g; Fiber: 1.2g; Sugar: 2.9g; Fat 41% / Protein 50% / Carbs 9%

Classic Italian Baccala

Serves: 4 / Preparation time: 10 minutes / Cooking time: 30 minutes

12 oz cod, dried and salted

½ lemon juice

½ tsp red pepper flakes

¼ cup fresh parsley, chopped

1 1/3 cup tomatoes, chopped

½ cup white wine

1 garlic clove, chopped

½ onion, chopped

1 tbsp olive oil

- Soak fish in water for 4 hours. Drain well.
- Boil fish in fresh water for 20 minutes or until tender. Drain well and fake the fish.
- Heat oil in a pan over medium heat.
- Add garlic and onion and sauté until onion is softened.
- Add wine and tomatoes and cook for 3-4 minutes.
- Add parsley and cooked fish and cook for 1-2 minutes.
- Add lemon juice and red pepper flakes and stir well.
- Serve and enjoy.

Per Serving: Net Carbs: 4g; Calories: 165; Total Fat: 4.5g; Saturated Fat: 0.7g
Protein: 20.4g; Carbs: 5.2g; Fiber: 1.2g; Sugar: 2.6g; Fat 32% / Protein 57% / Carbs 11%

Parmesan Cod

Serves: 4 / Preparation time: 10 minutes / Cooking time: 20 minutes

1 lb cod, cut into 4 pieces

4 tbsp butter

1 tbsp dried parsley

1 tsp dried oregano

1 tbsp fresh lemon juice

1 tsp garlic, minced

¾ cup parmesan cheese, grated

- Preheat the oven to 400 F/ 200 C.
- Add garlic and butter in microwave-safe bowl and microwave until butter is melted. Add lemon juice and stir well.
- Mix together parmesan cheese, parsley, and oregano in a shallow dish.
- Dip cod pieces into the butter mixture then coat with cheese mixture and place on a baking tray.
- Bake in preheated oven for 20 minutes.
- Serve and enjoy.

Per Serving: Net Carbs: 0.4g; Calories: 374; Total Fat: 21.6g; Saturated Fat: 13.5g
Protein: 38.2g; Carbs: 0.6g; Fiber: 0.2g; Sugar: 0.1g; Fat 55% / Protein 44% / Carbs 1%

Lemon Scungilli Salad

Serves: 6 / Preparation time: 10 minutes / Cooking time: 5 minutes

28 oz can scungilli

1/8 tsp celery seed

3 tbsp fresh lemon juice

¼ cup olive oil

2 garlic cloves, sliced

4 oz olives, sliced

¼ cup fresh parsley, chopped

1 cup celery, sliced

Pepper

Salt

- Add all ingredients into the large mixing bowl and toss well.
- Season salad with pepper and salt.
- Serve and enjoy.

Per Serving: Net Carbs: 3.8g; Calories: 209 Total Fat: 10.6g; Saturated Fat: 1.5g
Protein: 22.1g; Carbs: 4.8g; Fiber: 1g; Sugar: 0.4g; Fat 48% / Protein 45% / Carbs 7%

VEGETARIAN RECIPES

Contents

Delicious Ratatouille

Serves: 8 / Preparation time: 10 minutes / Cooking time: 4 hours

1 cup fresh basil, chopped

¼ tsp red pepper flakes

1 tsp dried oregano

2 tbsp tomato paste

1 cup cherry tomatoes, chopped

2 summer squash, sliced

1 bell pepper, chopped

1 eggplant, chopped

1 tbsp garlic, minced

1 onion, chopped

2 tbsp olive oil

¼ tsp pepper

½ tsp sea salt

- Add all ingredients except basil into the slow cooker and stir well.
- Cover and cook on high for 4 hours.
- Stir and serve.

Per Serving: Net Carbs: 6.6g; Calories: 79; Total Fat: 3.9g; Saturated Fat: 0.6g
Protein: 2.6g; Carbs: 10.9g; Fiber: 4.3g; Sugar: 5.9g; Fat 48% / Protein 17% / Carbs 35%

Light Mediterranean Salad

Serves: 6 / Preparation time: 10 minutes / Cooking time: 5 minutes

8 oz feta cheese, crumbled

½ onion, sliced

3 medium cucumber, peeled and chopped

2 tomatoes, chopped

4 cups salad greens

- In a large bowl, layer salad greens, onion, cucumber, tomatoes, and feta cheese.
- Serve and enjoy.

Per Serving: Net Carbs: 5.3g; Calories: 109; Total Fat: 5.7g; Saturated Fat: 3.4g
Protein: 8.1g; Carbs: 7g; Fiber: 1.7g; Sugar: 2.9g; Fat 49% / Protein 31% / Carbs 20%

Eggplant Salad

Serves: 12 / Preparation time: 10 minutes / Cooking time: 1 hour 30 minutes

5 eggplants

¼ tsp dried basil

1 tsp dried oregano

1 tsp dried parsley

1 tbsp balsamic vinegar

3 tbsp olive oil

1 garlic clove, crushed

Pepper

Salt

- Preheat the oven to 175 C/ 350 F.
- Pierce eggplant with a fork and place on a baking tray and bake in preheated oven for 1 hour 30 minutes or until soft.
- Remove eggplant from oven and let it cool completely then peel and diced.
- Transfer eggplant into the mixing bowl. Add remaining ingredients and mix well.
- Place in refrigerator for 2 hours.
- Serve and enjoy.

Per Serving: Net Carbs: 5.5g; Calories: 88 Total Fat: 3.9g; Saturated Fat: 0.5g
Protein: 2.3g; Carbs: 13.6g; Fiber: 8.1g; Sugar: 6.9g; Fat 50% / Protein 20% / Carbs 30%

Cauliflower Carrot Soup

Serves: 8 / Preparation time: 10 minutes / Cooking time: 25 minutes

1 cauliflower head, chopped

4 carrots, shredded

1 tbsp olive oil

1 tbsp curry powder

1 tsp turmeric powder

1 tbsp ginger, grated

8 cups vegetable broth

1 onion, diced

6 oz coconut milk

¼ tsp red pepper flakes

Pepper

Salt

- Heat olive oil in a large saucepan over medium heat.
- Add onion and sauté for 5 minutes.
- Add cauliflower, red pepper flakes, carrots, and broth and bring to boil. Turn heat to low and simmer until vegetables are softened.
- Add curry powder, turmeric, and ginger and stir well.
- Puree the soup using a blender until smooth.
- Add coconut milk and stir well. Season soup with pepper and salt.
- Serve and enjoy.

Per Serving: Net Carbs: 6.5g; Calories: 120; Total Fat: 6.7g; Saturated Fat: 4.9g
Protein: 6.6g; Carbs: 9.3g; Fiber: 2.8g; Sugar: 4.4g; Fat 53% / Protein 25% / Carbs 22%

Roasted Broccoli

Serves: 6 / Preparation time: 10 minutes / Cooking time: 20 minutes

4 cups broccoli florets

½ tsp garlic powder

1 tsp Italian seasoning

3 tbsp olive oil

½ tsp pepper

1 tsp salt

- Preheat the oven to 200 C/ 400 F.

- Spray a baking tray with cooking spray.

- Spread broccoli on a baking tray and drizzle with oil and season with garlic powder, Italian seasoning, pepper, and salt.

- Bake in preheated oven for 15-20 minutes.

- Serve and enjoy.

Per Serving: Net Carbs: 2.7g; Calories: 84; Total Fat: 7.4g; Saturated Fat: 1g
Protein: 1.8g; Carbs: 4.4g; Fiber: 1.7g; Sugar: 1.2g; Fat 80% / Protein 8% / Carbs 12%

Lemon Cauliflower Salad

Serves: 4 / Preparation time: 10 minutes / Cooking time: 10 minutes

1 cauliflower head, cut into florets

¼ tsp red pepper flakes

¼ cup fresh parsley, chopped

2 tbsp capers

¼ cup fresh lemon juice

1 lemon zest

2 small anchovies

½ cup olive oil

1 garlic clove

Pepper

Salt

- Add 2 cups of water and cauliflower into the saucepan. Cover and cook over high heat for 6-10 minutes or until softened. Drain well and transfer in large bowl.

- Add garlic, lemon juice, olive oil, and anchovies into the blender and blend until smooth.

- Pour blended mixture, capers, lemon zest, parsley, red pepper flakes, pepper, and salt over cauliflower and toss to coat.

- Serve and enjoy.

Per Serving: Net Carbs: 3.5g; Calories: 249 Total Fat: 25.7g; Saturated Fat: 3.8g
Protein: 2.4g; Carbs: 6g; Fiber: 2.5g; Sugar: 2.3g; Fat 92% / Protein 3% / Carbs 5%

Cucumber Lettuce Pepper Salad

Serves: 6 / Preparation time: 10 minutes / Cooking time: 5 minutes

1 small cucumber, chopped

1 carrot, sliced

2 tomatoes, diced

1 tsp garlic, minced

1 tsp fresh oregano, minced

1 tbsp apple cider vinegar

2 tbsp olive oil

2 tbsp fresh lemon juice

½ cup pepperoncini, sliced

½ cup olives, chopped

1 roasted bell pepper, sliced

¼ cup feta cheese, crumbled

6 cups lettuce, chopped

Pepper

Salt

- Add all ingredients into the large mixing bowl and toss to mix well.

- Season salad with pepper and salt.

- Serve and enjoy.

Per Serving: Net Carbs: 5.8g; Calories: 100; Total Fat: 7.5g; Saturated Fat: 1.8g
Protein: 2.1g; Carbs: 7.7g; Fiber: 1.9g; Sugar: 1.9g; Fat 68% / Protein 9% / Carbs 23%

Italain Eggplant Curry

Serves: 8 / Preparation time: 10 minutes / Cooking time: 27 minutes

2 lbs eggplant, diced

1 cup half and half

1 tsp mustard seeds

1 tsp cumin seeds

1 tsp curry powder

½ tsp turmeric powder

1 tsp apple cider vinegar

1 tbsp garlic, minced

2 tbsp olive oil

1 green chilies, sliced

1 onion, diced

Pepper

Salt

- Heat oil in a medium saucepan over medium heat.
- Once the oil is hot then add mustard seeds and cumin seeds and sauté for 30 seconds.
- Add eggplant and sauté for 8-10 minutes.
- Add garlic, green chili, and onion and sauté for 2-3 minutes.
- Add turmeric, curry powder, pepper, and salt and cook for 1 minute.
- Add vinegar and cook for 3-5 minutes.
- Add half and half and cook for 5-7 minutes.
- Stir well and serve over cauliflower rice.

Per Serving: Net Carbs: 5.6g; Calories: 94; Total Fat: 5.7g; Saturated Fat: 2.4g
Protein: 2.4g; Carbs: 10.1g; Fiber: 4.5g; Sugar: 4.1g; Fat 59% / Protein 16% / Carbs 25%

oasted Cauliflower with Red Bell Pepper

Serves: 4 / Preparation time: 10 minutes / Cooking time: 30 minutes

1 cauliflower head, cut into florets

2 tsp olive oil

2 tbsp white wine vinegar

3 tbsp balsamic vinegar

½ cup fresh dill, chopped

½ onion, sliced

1 red bell pepper, cut into 1-inch pieces

Pepper

Salt

- Add all ingredients into the zip-lock bag. Seal bag and shake well and place in the refrigerator for 1 hour.

- Preheat the oven to 232 C/ 450 F.

- Pour marinated cauliflower mixture in the baking dish and bake in preheated oven for 30 minutes.

- Serve and enjoy.

Per Serving: Net Carbs: 6.4g; Calories: 66 Total Fat: 2.7g; Saturated Fat: 0.4g
Protein: 2.9g; Carbs: 9.7g; Fiber: 3.3g; Sugar: 3.2g; Fat 39% / Protein 20% / Carbs 41%

Perfect Summer Salad

Serves: 3 / Preparation time: 10 minutes / Cooking time: 5 minutes

For salad:

½ cup tomatoes, chopped

½ cup hearts of palm, chopped

½ cup artichoke hearts, chopped

½ cup cucumber, chopped

1 tsp fresh basil, chopped

½ avocado, chopped

1 tbsp capers, chopped

2 tbsp onion, chopped

2 tbsp olives, chopped

For dressing:

¼ cup olive oil

¼ cup fresh lemon juice

Salt

- In a small bowl, whisk together all dressing ingredients and set aside.
- Add all salad ingredients into the mixing bowl and mix well.
- Pour dressing over salad and toss well.
- Serve and enjoy.

Per Serving: Net Carbs: 4.6g; Calories: 250; Total Fat: 24.4g; Saturated Fat: 4.1g
Protein: 2.7g; Carbs: 9.4g; Fiber: 4.8g; Sugar: 2.3g; Fat 88% / Protein 5% / Carbs 7%

Roasted Asparagus

Serves: 4 / Preparation time: 10 minutes / Cooking time: 12 minutes

1 lb asparagus, wash, trimmed, and cut the ends

3 oz parmesan cheese, shaved

1 tsp dried oregano

1 tbsp dried parsley

2 garlic cloves, minced

2 tbsp olive oil

Pepper

Salt

- Preheat the oven to 218 C/ 425 F.

- Spray a baking tray with cooking spray.

- Arrange asparagus on a baking tray. Drizzle olive oil over asparagus and season with pepper and salt.

- Spread cheese, oregano, parsley, and garlic over asparagus and bake in preheated oven for 10-12 minutes.

- Serve and enjoy.

Per Serving: Net Carbs: 3.4g; Calories: 155; Total Fat: 11.8g; Saturated Fat: 4.1g
Protein: 9.5g; Carbs: 6g; Fiber: 2.6g; Sugar: 2.2g; Fat 68% / Protein 24% / Carbs 8%

Roasted Cauliflower & Tomatoes

Serves: 4 / Preparation time: 10 minutes / Cooking time: 20 minutes

4 cups cauliflower florets

2 tbsp fresh parsley, chopped

2 garlic cloves, sliced

1 tbsp capers, drained

3 tbsp olive oil

½ cup cherry tomatoes, halved

Pepper

Salt

- Preheat the oven to 232 C/ 450 F.

- In a bowl, toss together cherry tomatoes, cauliflower, oil, garlic, capers, pepper, and salt and spread on a baking tray.

- Roast in preheated oven for 20 minutes.

- Garnish with parsley and serve.

Per Serving: Net Carbs: 4g; Calories: 123 Total Fat: 10.7g; Saturated Fat: 1.5g
Protein: 2.4g; Carbs: 6.9g; Fiber: 2.9g; Sugar: 3g; Fat 79% / Protein 8% / Carbs 13%

Healthy Tomato Basil Soup

Serves: 6 / Preparation time: 10 minutes / Cooking time: 20 minutes

28 oz can tomatoes, diced

¼ cup fresh basil leaves

½ cup heavy cream

1 ½ cups vegetable stock

¼ tsp Italian seasoning

1 tsp garlic, minced

1 onion, chopped

2 tbsp butter

1 tbsp olive oil

Pepper

Salt

- Heat butter and oil in a medium saucepan over medium-high heat.

- Add onion and sauté for 5 minutes.

- Add garlic and sauté for 30 seconds.

- Add tomatoes, Italian seasoning, and broth and stir well. Bring to boil over high heat.

- Turn heat to medium-low and simmer for 8 minutes.

- Puree the soup using immersion blender until smooth.

- Stir in basil and heavy cream. Season soup with pepper and salt.

- Stir well and serve hot.

Per Serving: Net Carbs: 6.6g; Calories: 127; Total Fat: 10.3g; Saturated Fat: 5.4g
Protein: 1.7g; Carbs: 9.3g; Fiber: 2.7g; Sugar: 5.6g; Fat 73% / Protein 6% / Carbs 21%

Simple Greek Salad

Serves: 2 / Preparation time: 10 minutes / Cooking time: 5 minutes

1 cup lettuce, chopped

5 olives, chopped

¼ cup red bell pepper, diced

¼ cup tomato, diced

½ cup cucumber, diced

1 oz feta cheese, crumbled

For dressing:

2 tsp red wine vinegar

1 tbsp olive oil

¼ tsp dried oregano

Pepper

Salt

- In a small bowl, mix together all dressing ingredients and set aside.
- Add remaining ingredients into the mixing bowl and mix well.
- Pour dressing over salad and toss well.
- Serve and enjoy.

Per Serving: Net Carbs: 4.1g; Calories: 128; Total Fat: 11.4g; Saturated Fat: 3.3g
Protein: 2.8g; Carbs: 5.3g; Fiber: 1.2g; Sugar: 2.7g; Fat 80% / Protein 8% / Carbs 12%

Italian Bell Peppers

Serves: 4 / Preparation time: 10 minutes / Cooking time: 20 minutes

2 large bell peppers, seeded and sliced

1 tsp fresh oregano, chopped

4 garlic cloves, peeled

¼ onion, sliced

¼ tsp red pepper flakes

1 tbsp olive oil

1 tbsp basil, chopped

Pepper

Salt

- Heat oil in a pan over medium heat.

- Add garlic and sauté for 3-5 minutes or until garlic caramelize.

- Add onion, peppers, red pepper flakes, pepper, and salt and cook over medium-high heat for 15 minutes.

- Garnish with basil and serve.

Per Serving: Net Carbs: 5.3g; Calories: 58 Total Fat: 3.7g; Saturated Fat: 0.5g
Protein: 0.9g; Carbs: 6.5g; Fiber: 1.2g; Sugar: 3.4g; Fat 57% / Protein 7% / Carbs 36%

Roasted Cauliflower & Mushrooms

Serves: 6 / Preparation time: 10 minutes / Cooking time: 20 minutes

1 lb mushrooms, cleaned

1 tbsp fresh parsley, chopped

1 tbsp Italian seasoning

2 tbsp olive oil

10 garlic cloves, peeled

2 cups cherry tomatoes

2 cups cauliflower florets

Pepper

Salt

- Preheat the oven to 200 C/ 400 F.
- Add cauliflower, mushrooms, Italian seasoning, olive oil, garlic, cherry tomatoes, pepper, and salt into the mixing bowl and toss well.
- Transfer cauliflower and mushroom mixture on a baking tray and roast in preheated oven for 25-30 minutes.
- Garnish with parsley and serve.

Per Serving: Net Carbs: 6g; Calories: 90; Total Fat: 5.8g; Saturated Fat: 0.8g
Protein: 3.9g; Carbs: 8.5g; Fiber: 2.5g; Sugar: 3.9g; Fat 57% / Protein 17% / Carbs 26%

Sauteed Mushrooms

Serves: 6 / Preparation time: 10 minutes / Cooking time: 1 minute

1 lb mushrooms, sliced

1 red bell pepper, sliced

½ onion, diced

¾ cup Italian dressing

2 tbsp fresh parsley, chopped

Pepper

Salt

- Spray pan with cooking spray and heat over medium-high heat.
- Add mushrooms and salt and sauté for 5-7 minutes.
- Add red bell pepper, onion, and Italian dressing and bring to boil.
- Turn heat to medium and cook for 3 minutes.
- Season with pepper and salt.
- Garnish with parsley and serve.

Per Serving: Net Carbs: 6.2g; Calories: 110; Total Fat: 8.6g; Saturated Fat: 1.3g
Protein: 2.8g; Carbs: 7.5g; Fiber: 1.3g; Sugar: 4.8g; Fat 70% / Protein 9% / Carbs 21%

Flavors Eggplant & Zucchini

Serves: 6 / Preparation time: 10 minutes / Cooking time: 5 hours

1 lb eggplant, peeled and cut 1-inch cubes

3 oz feta cheese, crumbled

2 tsp dried basil

1 tbsp garlic, minced

1 zucchini, chopped

3 fresh tomatoes, diced

1/2 onion, diced

1 red bell pepper, chopped

1 tbsp olive oil

Pepper

Salt

- Add all ingredients except feta cheese into the slow cooker and stir well.
- Cover and cook on low for 5 hours.
- Top with crumbled cheese and serve.

Per Serving: Net Carbs: 6.6g; Calories: 103 Total Fat: 5.7g; Saturated Fat: 2.5g
Protein: 4.1g; Carbs: 10.9g; Fiber: 4.3g; Sugar: 6.1g; Fat 54% / Protein 19% / Carbs 27%

Refreshing Cucumber Salad

Serves: 6 / Preparation time: 10 minutes / Cooking time: 5 minutes

2 cucumber, sliced

½ cup feta cheese, crumbled

¼ cup fresh dill, chopped

1 small onion, sliced

For dressing:

¼ cup mayonnaise

½ cup Greek yogurt

2 tbsp white vinegar

¼ tsp pepper

¼ tsp salt

- In a small bowl, mix together all dressing ingredients and set aside.
- Add remaining ingredients into the mixing bowl and mix well.
- Pour dressing over salad and toss well.
- Serve and enjoy.

Per Serving: Net Carbs: 6.9g; Calories: 134; Total Fat: 9.8g; Saturated Fat: 3.1g
Protein: 4.1g; Carbs: 7.9g; Fiber: 1g; Sugar: 318g; Fat 66% / Protein 13% / Carbs 21%

Grilled Zucchini

Serves: 4 / Preparation time: 10 minutes / Cooking time: 10 minute

3 medium zucchinis, cut lengthwise

½ cup feta cheese, crumbled

2 tbsp Greek seasoning

2 tbsp olive oil

Pepper

Salt

- Coat zucchini with olive oil and season with Greek seasoning, pepper, and salt.

- Preheat the grill.

- Arrange zucchini on hot grill and cook for 3 minutes.

- Turn zucchini to the other side and cook for 3 minutes. Turn zucchini green skin side down and cook for 3 minutes more.

- Arrange grilled zucchini on serving plate and top with crumbled cheese.

- Serve and enjoy.

Per Serving: Net Carbs: 6.4g; Calories: 144; Total Fat: 11.4g; Saturated Fat: 3.9g
Protein: 4.7g; Carbs: 8g; Fiber: 1.6g; Sugar: 3.3g; Fat 70% / Protein 13% / Carbs 17%

\

DESSERTS RECIPES

Contents

Blackberry Yogurt

Serves: 6 / Preparation time: 5 minutes / Cooking time: 5 minutes

4 cups frozen unsweetened blackberries   1 cup yogurt

1 tsp vanilla

1 tbsp fresh lemon juice

- Add all ingredients into the blender and blend until smooth.
- Pour blended mixture into the air-tight container and place in the refrigerator for 2 hours.
- Serve and enjoy.

Per Serving: Net Carbs: 5.7g; Calories: 48 Total Fat: 0.6g; Saturated Fat: 0.4g
Protein: 2.6g; Carbs: 7g; Fiber: 1.3g; Sugar: 5.7g; Fat 18% / Protein 27% / Carbs 55%

Lemon Yogurt Muffins

Serves: 12 / Preparation time: 10 minutes / Cooking time: 15 minutes

2 eggs

2 tbsp poppy seeds

1 tsp baking powder, gluten-free

¼ cup coconut flour

1 cup almond flour

1/3 cup swerve

1 fresh lemon juice

1 tbsp lemon zest

1/3 cup butter, melted

½ cup yogurt

- Preheat the oven to 180 C/ 350 F.
- Spray a muffin tray with cooking spray and set aside.
- Add all ingredients into the mixing bowl and mix until well combined.
- Pour batter into the prepared muffin tray and bake in preheated oven for 12-15 minutes.
- Serve and enjoy.

Per Serving: Net Carbs: 3g; Calories: 139; Total Fat: 11.3g; Saturated Fat: 4.2g
Protein: 4.2g; Carbs: 5.2g; Fiber: 2.2g; Sugar: 1.1g; Fat 75% / Protein 15% / Carbs 10%

Strawberry Granita

Serves: 8 / Preparation time: 10 minutes / Cooking time: 5 minutes

2 lbs strawberries, halved

1 tsp liquid stevia

¼ tsp balsamic vinegar

½ tsp fresh lemon juice

1 cup of water

Pinch of salt

- Add all ingredients into the blender and blend until smooth.

- Pour blended mixture into the baking dish and place it in the freezer for 45 minutes.

- After 45 minutes lightly stir the granite mixture using a fork and again place in the freezer for 40 minutes more.

- Again stir granite using a fork and serve.

Per Serving: Net Carbs: 6.4g; Calories: 36; Total Fat: 0.3g; Saturated Fat: 0g
Protein: 0.8g; Carbs: 8.7g; Fiber: 2.3g; Sugar: 5.6g; Fat 14% / Protein 15% / Carbs 71%

Orange Yogurt Pops

Serves: 4 / Preparation time: 5 minutes / Cooking time: 5 minutes

½ cup of orange juice   ½ cup vanilla yogurt

- In a bowl, whisk together yogurt and orange juice.
- Pour into the Popsicle molds and place them in the refrigerator until set.
- Serve and enjoy.

Per Serving: Net Carbs: 5.3g; Calories: 36 Total Fat: 0.4g; Saturated Fat: 0.3g
Protein: 2g; Carbs: 5.4g; Fiber: 0.1g; Sugar: 4.8g; Fat 16% / Protein 26% / Carbs 58%

Peach Fat Bombs

Serves: 8 / Preparation time: 10 minutes / Cooking time: 10 minutes

4 oz cream cheese

1 tsp peach extract

2 tbsp Swerve

¼ cup coconut flour

2 oz butter, softened

For coating:

¼ tsp ground cinnamon

2 tbsp almond flour

- Add cream cheese, peach extract, swerve, coconut flour, and butter into the food processor and process until well combined and place in the refrigerator for 15 minutes.

- In a shallow dish, mix together almond flour and cinnamon.

- Remove cream cheese mixture from the refrigerator. Make small balls from cheese mixture and roll in almond flour mixture.

- Serve and enjoy.

Per Serving: Net Carbs: 2.1g; Calories: 127; Total Fat: 11.9g; Saturated Fat: 7.1g
Protein: 2g; Carbs: 3.8g; Fiber: 1.7g; Sugar: 0g; Fat 85% / Protein 7% / Carbs 8%

Blueberry Yogurt Muffins

Serves: 12 / Preparation time: 10 minutes / Cooking time: 30 minutes

5.5 oz plain yogurt

½ cup fresh blueberries

2 tsp baking powder, gluten-free

¼ cup Swerve

2 ½ cups almond flour

½ tsp vanilla

3 eggs

Pinch of salt

- Preheat the oven to 162 C/ 325 F.
- Spray a muffin tray with cooking spray and set aside.
- In a bowl, whisk together yogurt, vanilla, eggs, and salt until smooth.
- Add almond flour, baking powder, and swerve and blend again until smooth.
- Add blueberries and stir well. Pour batter into the prepared muffin tray.
- Bake in preheated oven for 25-30 minutes.
- Serve and enjoy.

Per Serving: Net Carbs: 4.6g; Calories: 165; Total Fat: 13.1g; Saturated Fat: 1.4g
Protein: 7.4g; Carbs: 7.3g; Fiber: 2.7g; Sugar: 2.5g; Fat 72% / Protein 17% / Carbs 11%

Lemon Flavor Cheesecake Mousse

Serves: 8 / Preparation time: 10 minutes / Cooking time: 5 minutes

8 oz cream cheese

1/3 cup Swerve

2/3 cup lemon curd

1 cup heavy cream

- Add heavy cream in a large bowl and whip until soft peaks form.
- In a separate bowl, whip cream cheese until smooth. Add swerve and lemon curd and whip until combined.
- Pour cream cheese mixture into the heavy cream and mix until combined.
- Place mousse in the freezer for 15 minutes before serving.

Per Serving: Net Carbs: 6.6g; Calories: 231 Total Fat: 23.4g; Saturated Fat: 13.7g
Protein: 3.8g; Carbs: 6.6g; Fiber: 0g; Sugar: 5.4g; Fat 88% / Protein 4% / Carbs 8%

Chocolate Mousse

Serves: 4 / Preparation time: 5 minutes / Cooking time: 5 minutes

1 ½ cups heavy whipping cream

1/3 cup unsweetened cocoa powder

2 tbsp Swerve

- Add heavy whipping cream in mixing bowl and whip until thickens.
- Add cocoa powder and swerve and whip again until stiff peaks form.
- Pour in container and place in the refrigerator for 2 hours.
- Serve and enjoy.

Per Serving: Net Carbs: 3.8g; Calories: 174; Total Fat: 17.6g; Saturated Fat: 10.9g
Protein: 2.3g; Carbs: 6.2g; Fiber: 2.4g; Sugar: 0.2g; Fat 89% / Protein 4% / Carbs 7%

Coconut Avocado Popsicles

Serves: 6 / Preparation time: 5 minutes / Cooking time: 5 minute

2 avocados, pitted

2 tbsp fresh lime juice

¼ cup Swerve

1 ½ cups coconut milk

- Add all ingredients into the blender and blend until smooth.
- Pour into the Popsicle molds and place them in the freezer until set.
- Serve and enjoy.

Per Serving: Net Carbs: 2.1g; Calories: 169; Total Fat: 16.1g; Saturated Fat: 5.2g
Protein: 1.6g; Carbs: 6.6g; Fiber: 4.5g; Sugar: 0.3g; Fat 87% / Protein 6% / Carbs 7%

Lemon Raspberry Popsicles

Serves: 10 / Preparation time: 5 minutes / Cooking time: 5 minutes

½ cup frozen raspberries, chopped

5 drops liquid stevia

2 cups of water

1 cup fresh lemon juice

- Evenly divide chopped raspberries into the Popsicle molds.

- In a bowl, whisk together lemon juice, water, and stevia and pour into the Popsicle mold.

- Place in refrigerator until set.

- Serve and enjoy.

Per Serving: Net Carbs: 3.1g; Calories: 19 Total Fat: 0.2g; Saturated Fat: 0.2g
Protein: 0.3g; Carbs: 3.8g; Fiber: 0.7g; Sugar: 3.2g; Fat 18% / Protein 15% / Carbs 67%

THE "DIRTY DOZEN" AND "CLEAN 15"

Every year, the Environmental Working Group releases a list of the produce with the most pesticide residue (Dirty Dozen) and a list of the ones with the least **chance of having residue (Clean 15). It's based on analysis from the U.S.** Department of Agriculture Pesticide Data Program report.

The Environmental Working Group found that 70% of the 48 types of produce tested had residues of at least one type of pesticide. In total there were 178 different pesticides and pesticide breakdown products. This residue can stay on veggies and fruit even after they are washed and peeled. All pesticides are toxic to humans and consuming them can cause damage to the nervous system, reproductive system, cancer, a weakened immune system, and more. Women who are pregnant can expose their unborn children to toxins through their diet, and continued exposure to pesticides can affect their development.

This info can help you choose the best fruits and veggies, as well as which ones you should always try to buy organic.

The Dirty Dozen

- Strawberries
- Spinach
- Nectarines
- Apples
- Peaches
- Celery
- Grapes
- Pears
- Cherries
- Tomatoes
- Sweet bell peppers
- Potatoes

The Clean 15

- Sweet corn
- Avocados
- Pineapples
- Cabbage
- Onions
- Frozen sweet peas
- Papayas
- Asparagus
- Mangoes
- Eggplant
- Honeydew
- Kiwi
- Cantaloupe
- Cauliflower
- Grapefruit

MEASUREMENT CONVERSION TABLES

VOLUME EQUIVALENTS (DRY)

US Standard	Metric (Approx.)
¼ teaspoon	1 ml
½ teaspoon	2 ml
1 teaspoon	5 ml
1 tablespoon	15 ml
¼ cup	59 ml
½ cup	118 ml
1 cup	235 ml

WEIGHT EQUIVALENTS

US Standard	Metric (Approx.)
½ ounce	15 g
1 ounce	30 g
2 ounces	60 g
4 ounces	115 g
8 ounces	225 g
12 ounces	340 g
16 oz or 1 lb	455 g

VOLUME EQUIVALENTS (LIQUID)

US Standard	US Standard (ounces)	Metric (Approx.)
2 tablespoons	1 fl oz	30 ml
¼ cup	2 fl oz	60 ml
½ cup	4 fl oz	120 ml
1 cup	8 fl oz	240 ml
1 ½ cups	12 fl oz	355 ml
2 cups or 1 pint	16 fl oz	475 ml
4 cups or 1 quart	32 fl oz	1 L
1 gallon	128 fl oz	4 L

OVEN TEMPERATURES

Fahrenheit (F)	Celsius (C) (Approx)
250°F	120°C
300°F	150°C
325°F	165°C
350°F	180°C
375°F	190°C
400°F	200°C
425°F	220°C
450°F	230°C

INDEX

Manufactured by Amazon.ca
Bolton, ON

21768146R00074